21 世纪高等学校物流管理与物流工程规划教材

物流管理案例与分析
（双语版）

主编 阚功俭 张媛媛

清华大学出版社
北京交通大学出版社
·北京·

内 容 简 介

本书共编写了 29 个英文案例，分为八个模块：采购与供应商管理、物流营销管理、运输管理、仓储与库存管理、物流信息管理、供应链管理、国际物流和整合物流管理。每个案例之后安排了英文讨论题和案例分析提示、中文的术语解释和案例概述，有助于读者迅速、准确地把握本模块的基本内容并拓展思路，学以致用。本书可作为普通高等院校物流管理、工商管理等专业硕士生与本科生的教材和参考用书，也可作为国际商务与国际物流管理人员的培训参考用书。

本书封面贴有清华大学出版社防伪标签，无标签者不得销售。
版权所有，侵权必究。侵权举报电话：010-62782989　13501256678　13801310933

图书在版编目（CIP）数据

物流管理案例与分析：双语版 / 阚功俭，张媛媛主编. —北京：北京交通大学出版社：清华大学出版社，2021.1

21 世纪高等学校物流管理与物流工程规划教材

ISBN 978-7-5121-4370-8

Ⅰ. ① 物… Ⅱ. ① 阚… ② 张… Ⅲ. ① 物流–物资管理–双语教学–高等学校–教材–汉、英 Ⅳ. ① F252

中国版本图书馆 CIP 数据核字（2020）第 231262 号

物流管理案例与分析（双语版）
WULIU GUANLI ANLI YU FENXI (SHUANGYUBAN)

策划编辑：陈建峰　　责任编辑：吴嫦娥	
出版发行：清 华 大 学 出 版 社　邮编：100084　电话：010-62776969　http://www.tup.com.cn	
北京交通大学出版社　邮编：100044　电话：010-51686414　http://www.bjtup.com.cn	
印　刷　者：北京鑫海金澳胶印有限公司	
经　　　销：全国新华书店	
开　　　本：185 mm×260 mm　　印张：11.5　　字数：294 千字	
版 印 次：2021 年 1 月第 1 版　2021 年 1 月第 1 次印刷	
定　　　价：49.00 元	

本书如有质量问题，请向北京交通大学出版社质监组反映。对您的意见和批评，我们表示欢迎和感谢。
投诉电话：010-51686043，51686008；传真：010-62225406；E-mail：press@bjtu.edu.cn。

物流学自20世纪初产生以来在世界范围内受到广泛重视并得到迅速发展，是一门由经济学、管理学、工学和理学等互相交叉形成的新兴学科。随着我国经济体制改革的深入和经济全球化的发展，物流成为国民经济的重要产业和新的经济增长点。20多年来，随着案例教学法得到更多管理学院、管理教师的认可，中国物流管理教育对于案例的需求日益旺盛，从事物流管理与物流工程教育的广大教师也非常希望能看到更多有关国内外物流管理案例和案例分析方法的书籍。目前市面上已经出现了许多中文案例或附带国外案例的英文版物流图书，但是在案例的时效性、针对性与提高读者的英文理解能力和实际案例分析能力方面做得不尽人意。本书搜集了欧美国家代表性的时新案例，通过对西方先进国家物流企业管理案例的解析提高读者的英语阅读能力、综合分析能力和创新思维能力。作者联合美国阿肯色州立大学的运营管理专任教师John Seydel教授，结合多年的物流专业英语和物流企业管理双语课程的教学实践，力争呈现给读者一本结构清晰、内容丰富、实践性强的物流管理英文案例教材。同以往的物流案例教材相比，本教材具有以下特色。

首先，所有案例均为纯英文的物流管理实践案例，有利于读者提高专业英语表达能力。

其次，每个部分的学习目标与各个案例的思考题有助于读者迅速、准确地把握本模块的基本内容并拓展思路。

再次，每个案例之后配有中文的术语解释与案例概述，易于学习掌握。

最后，书中的大部分案例在教学过程中已经多次使用，并取得了很好的教学效果。每个案例之后的英文案例分析提示浅显易懂，有助于启发读者思维，同时便于教师开展案例教学。

本书共分为八个部分，涵盖了八大模块。第一部分是采购与供应商管理，包括三个案例；第二部分是物流营销管理，包括三个案例；第三部分是运输管理，包括三个案例；第四部分是仓储与库存管理，包括三个案例；第五部分是物流信息管理，包括四个案例；第六部分是供应链管理，包括三个案例；第七部分是国际物流，包括四个案例；第八部分是整合物流管理，包括六个案例；附录部分是"案例分析与案例讨论指南"，旨在拓宽读者案例教学与案例分析的思路。

本书可作为普通高等院校物流管理和工商管理等专业的研究生与本科生案例教学使用的教材和参考用书，也可作为国际商务与国际物流管理人员的培训参考用书。全书的具体编写分工如下：阚功俭：Part One 的 Case 1，Case 2；Part Two；Part Three 的 Case 7，Case 8；Part Four；Part Five；Part Six 的 Case 17，Case 19；Part Seven 的 Case 21，Case 22；

I

Part Eight 的 Case 24，Case 25，Case 28。张媛媛：Part Three 的 Case 9，Part Six 的 Case 18；Part Seven 的 Case 20，Case 23；Part Eight 的 Case 27。John Seydel：Part One 的 Case 3；Part Eight 的 Case 26。阚成章：Part Eight 的 Case 29；王福华、邹霞、罗艳芳参与修改了 Part Three，Part Four 与 Part Eight 的部分内容。阚功俭、张媛媛负责全书的结构设计，阚功俭负责最后的统稿、定稿。

  本书在编写过程中参考了国内外专家学者的有关研究成果和文献，在此特向这些作者表示衷心感谢。同时北京交通大学出版社的编辑也为本书的出版付出了辛勤劳动，在此向他们表示崇高的敬意。由于物流管理案例涵盖范围很广，物流的理论和实践都处在不断发展和探索过程中，尽管我们为编写此书付出了巨大的努力，但由于水平有限，书中难免存在一些疏漏和错误，恳请专家与广大读者批评指正。

编　者

2020 年 9 月 25 日

Contents

Part One Procurement and Supplier Management ········ 1

- Case 1 Toyota's supplier relationship management ········ 3
- Case 2 Chemstar and Loftech ········ 9
- Case 3 FBK Industries: Supporting the Paradigm Shift in Vendor Selection through the Use of Multicriteria Methods for Sole-Sourcing ········ 12

Part Two Logistics Marketing Management ········ 27

- Case 4 UPS and FedEx turn focus to consumer behavior ········ 29
- Case 5 Handy Tider, Inc. ········ 35
- Case 6 DHL Logistics's Services Marketing Mix Efforts ········ 41

Part Three Transportation Management ········ 49

- Case 7 Coals to Newcastle ········ 51
- Case 8 H. Stevens Inc. ········ 55
- Case 9 Ocean spray-shipping products more efficiently ········ 59

Part Four Warehousing and Inventory Management ········ 63

- Case 10 Implementing CMI at the Whitbread Beer Company ········ 65
- Case 11 Healthy & handsome Trading ········ 70
- Case 12 Freshy company ········ 75

Part Five Logistics Information Management ········ 79

- Case 13 Care-free Hut ········ 81
- Case 14 WorthPal Inc. ········ 85
- Case 15 Supply-Base Reduction at Rabbity ········ 89
- Case 16 Enterprise-Level Coordination at Zappos ········ 92

Part Six	Supply Chain Management	97
Case 17	Managing Growth at SportStuff	99
Case 18	Birth of a Sweater	104
Case 19	Dell Computers: using the supply chain to compete	108

Part Seven	International Logistics	115
Case 20	Where to produce?	117
Case 21	Betty's Brownies	120
Case 22	The Great Bite Peach Company	124
Case 23	Two Countries Compared: Switzerland and Chad	129

Part Eight	Integrated Logistics Management	133
Case 24	ESB	135
Case 25	Tastyfood	139
Case 26	Online Sales and Local Store Availability: Combining the Best of Both Worlds, or Not?	142
Case 27	Human resource management in Humanitarian Aid Supply Chains	145
Case 28	Fast Fashion Winner from Savvy Systems	148
Case 29	LIDL Sweden	163

Appendix	A Guide to Case Analysis and Case Discussion	169
Part One	Objectives of Case Analysis	171
Part Two	How to prepare a Case for Class Discussion	172
Part Three	How to participate in Class Discussion of a Case	174

References	176

Part One

Procurement and Supplier Management

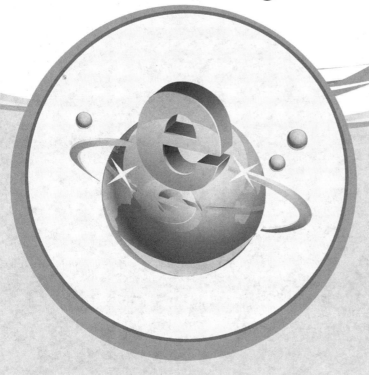

Part One Procurement and Supplier Management

Learning Objectives

After learning this part, you will be able to:
- Explain the role of procurement and supplier management
- Gain an understanding of purchasing process
- Identify areas for close coordination between purchasing and integrated logistics
- Apply supplier selection and evaluation techniques
- Understand the philosophy of supplier relationship management

Case 1

Toyota's supplier relationship management

In a field known for contentious manufacturer/supplier relationships, automotive giants Toyota and Honda have bucked the trend, leading the way in championing supplier relationships that go beyond just price. The Japanese concept of **keiretsu**[1], a close-knit network of vendors that continuously learn, improve, and prosper along with their parent companies, is the underlying strategy behind Honda and Toyota's supplier relationships. Other auto manufacturers — including the American heavyweights in Detroit — have failed miserably at attempts to establish similar practices. What's the secret to Toyota and Honda's success?

The simple answer is Honda and Toyota have turned arms-length relationships with suppliers into close partnerships, bringing increased efficiencies to both parties, says Choi, a professor of supply chain management at the W.P. Carey School of Business at ASU. The complex part is making that happen.

"Relationship-building is often overlooked as too mushy. Companies say, 'Why are you holding the supplier's hand? Why are you being so benevolent?'" says Choi. "But having a strong relationship with your suppliers actually has good, hard, solid business results." For Toyota and Honda, those results include faster production times than the majority of their U.S. competitors — they design new cars in just 12 to 18 months compared to the industry norm of two to three years. The automakers also reduced manufacturing costs on the Camry and the Accord, respectively — two of the three top-selling cars in the U.S.—by 25 percent in the 1990s, while still scoring top spots on the JD Powers customer satisfaction surveys.

During the last 10 to 15 years, the increased downsizing trend coupled with the spread of a truly global economy has led more and more companies to lean on suppliers to gain competitive edge. Outsourcing manufacturing operations to suppliers — when done successfully — can help businesses increase profit, time-to-market, and customer satisfaction, while decreasing costs and keeping up with consumer demand.

For Honda and Toyota, in particular, suppliers have been key to their innovation and success. Indeed, the two companies source about 70 to 80 percent of their manufacturing costs from outside suppliers. And suppliers return the favor: For example, many of the cost-cutting ideas that made Accord and Camry so successful came from suppliers. Of course, with such great reliance on suppliers comes a great need to manage and build relationships with those suppliers — and that is where the two Japanese automakers far outpace their American rivals. Though keiretsu was briefly in vogue with American business in the 1980s, its prominence was short-lived. "American companies decided the immediate benefits of low-wage costs outweighed the benefits of investing in relationships," says Choi.

It might be fair to assume the "cheaper, faster, better" American culture makes the concept of building deep supplier relationships alien to our way of conducting business. But Choi is quick to challenge that. Company culture, he says, is far more important.

"One need only look to the New United Motor Manufacturing Inc. (NUMMI) facility in Freemont, Calif., as an example," he says. The former GM facility suffered from labor management problems that threatened its existence when Toyota executives offered to revive the plant. Using the same facilities, equipment, and workers, Toyota implemented a keiretsu system with American managers and workers, with astounding success. Today, NUMMI is a Toyota/GM **joint venture**[2], and the manufacturing site for successful vehicles such as Toyota Corolla, Chevrolet Geo Prizm, and Toyota Takoma.

"Toyota proved that company culture matters," says Choi. "A lot of Honda and Toyota's good supplier-relationship practices can be transferred to American companies."

That is the good news for companies seeking to improve supplier relationships. The bad news? "If I were to summarize the key to building deep supplier relationships in one word, it would be 'diligence,'" says Choi.

Choi's findings — gleaned from interviews with more than 50 Toyota and Honda managers in Japan and the United States — show six best practices the two companies utilize to develop deep supplier relationships, namely, conduct joint improvement activities, share information intensively but selectively, develop suppliers' technical capabilities, supervise suppliers, turn supplier rivalry into opportunity, and understand how suppliers work. Toyota and Honda succeed by combining these elements together to form a supplier-partnering hierarchy.

Theirs is a "tough love" approach, with high standards and demanding requirements. It is tempered, however, by their belief that the supplier's success is absolutely crucial to their own.

Toyota and Honda's supply base cuts across different tiers — first-tier suppliers work with smaller, lower-tier suppliers to manufacture components according to Honda's specifications. Having multiple layers protects the automakers from supply chain exceptions, and provides depth and stability. "American manufacturers often have more flexibility since they typically use dozens of suppliers, but they are burdened with higher administrative costs, and no time to devote to relationship building," explains Choi.

A closer look at the practices in the supplier-partnering hierarchy shows Toyota and Honda's dedication to forming **deep supplier relationships**[3] — and the diligence it takes to manage them. Exchanging best practices, sharing information, honing innovation, and learning how suppliers work are all crucial parts of their process.

Target pricing, for example, is a constant gripe between manufacturers and suppliers, who often feel overburdened trying to meet manufacturers' constant cost reductions. Not so with Toyota and Honda. "When it comes to target pricing, Honda and Toyota do their homework," explains Choi. "They know what price the market can bear and they work backward, breaking down the cost one piece at a time. They also have a good idea about the suppliers' capability — can they meet this cost and still make money?" For worthy suppliers who cannot meet target prices, the automakers set up pricing schedules, giving suppliers three years, for example, to reduce the price of an item from $15 to $10.

Suppliers agree to this because they have faith the automakers will help them achieve the target prices, while making their own manufacturing prices leaner and more competitive.

When working with suppliers to develop technology, Toyota creates a guest engineer program — suppliers send engineers to Toyota's facilities to work alongside its own engineers for two or three years. This extensive training allows suppliers to fully integrate with the manufacturers' processes, and eventually, develop design ideas of their own. In addition, the experience makes the suppliers more technologically advanced, and increases their value to Toyota. Toyota doesn't seem worried about the **intellectual property**[4] these engineers carry with them after they leave. The company views its supplier relationship practices as "a competitive advantage that cannot easily be replicated in the marketplace," says Choi.

And the office swapping goes both ways. Honda, reports Choi, often sends its engineers — and occasionally its **senior executives**[5] — to suppliers' facilities to study their operations and cultures.

Extensive measuring systems — a common best practice among world-class supply chains — keep Honda's suppliers in check. Monthly reports measuring quality, delivery, and incident reports communicate performance to suppliers. When issues do arise, Honda expects senior management to be involved in resolution. Staying on top of supplier performance protects Honda's long-term investment in the supplier, and helps suppliers **benchmark**[6] their quality and develop new capabilities.

By helping suppliers better themselves in the process of meeting their exacting standards, Toyota and Honda create mutually beneficial relationships that allow them to get what they need from suppliers without beating them with a big stick. While American auto manufacturers have yet to find a way to do the same, Toyota and Honda's remarkable success with keiretsu has piqued much interest in the manufacturing world.

▶ Questions for discussion

1. What are the drawbacks of developing deep supplier relationships of a company with its suppliers?
2. What is Toyota's philosophy on working with suppliers?
3. What qualities does Toyota look for in existing and potential suppliers?
4. What advice would you offer to the senior executives of procurement in building long-term supplier relationships?

▶ New specialized terms

1. keiretsu   日本式的紧密联营公司
2. joint venture   合资企业
3. deep supplier relationship   密切的供应商关系
4. intellectual property   知识产权
5. senior executive   高管
6. benchmark   标准，基准

Case summary

丰田的供应商关系管理

在充满争议的生产商－供应商关系领域，汽车巨头丰田和本田引领行业潮流，超越了价格层次的竞争，在处理与其供应商的关系方面树立了典范。丰田和本田的供应商关系管理战略深受日本式的"紧密联营公司"观念的影响。在"紧密联营"的网络下，供应商不断学习、改进并依赖的母公司共同兴旺，而包括位于底特律的美国大牌在内的其他汽车制造商在供应商管理实践中却一败涂地。丰田和本田成功的秘诀何在？

阿肯色州立大学的供应链管理教授 Choi 认为，它们成功的理念很简单，就是把与供应商的关系从交易型转变为紧密伙伴型，真正复杂的是如何把理念付诸实施。通过建立密

切的供应商关系，丰田与本田将产品研制周期压缩到12~18个月，低于行业平均的2~3年。丰田凯美瑞与本田雅阁在20世纪90年代的制造成本分别降低了25%，而他们的客户满意度依然名列前茅。

过去的10~15年间，随着经济的日益全球化，企业规模不断缩减导致越来越多的公司依赖供应商提高其竞争力。成功地将制造业务外包给供应商有助于企业在降低制造成本、更好应对客户需求的同时，增加利润、提高市场反应速度与客户满意度。

丰田和本田的供应商对它们的创新与成功运营发挥了关键作用。例如，凯美瑞与雅阁的成功离不开降低成本的许多创意，而后者大多来自供应商。虽然20世纪80年代"紧密联营"的理念在美国也曾风靡一时，但好景不长。Choi 认为，美国公司更看重低工资带来的即刻效益而不是投资于建立良好的供应商关系。

客观地说，美国文化注重"更廉，更快，更好"，这使得"建立深入的供应商关系"理念有些不合时宜。Choi 却认为，企业文化远比短期利益重要。位于加州的新联合汽车制造商(NUMMI)是一个很好例证。在丰田高管提出振兴该厂的方案时，这个原通用汽车集团的配件厂因劳工管理问题一度陷入困境。面对同样的设施、设备与工人，丰田在美国经理与工人中实施"紧密联营"系统后大获成功。丰田的实践证明，企业文化很重要。Choi 认为，建立深入的供应商关系的关键可用一个词概括，那就是"勤奋"。Choi 通过对美国、日本的50家丰田、本田公司经理的访谈，发现了两家汽车集团用于维护良好供应商关系的六大最佳举措：施行联合改进计划；有选择地及时共享信息；培养供应商的技术能力；指导供应商；将对立型的供应商关系转变为机遇型的关系；了解供应商的工作流程。丰田和本田通过整合上述元素构筑供应商伙伴层级而取得了成功。因为对供应商的高标准、严要求，它们与供应商的联姻之路不乏障碍，但只要持有"供应商的成功对于它们自身的成功是至关重要"的信念，这种障碍很容易克服。

丰田和本田的供应商层级分明，各级供应商的数量少而精，这样既能保证供应的稳定性与灵活性，又便于建立和维护密切的供应商关系。通常拥有几十家供应商的美国制造商们，虽然选择供应商的余地很大，但受困于高昂的管理成本，几乎没有时间维护其供应商关系。

例如，制造商实行的"目标定价法"常常让其供应商为满足降低成本要求而陷入困境，这个问题在丰田和本田的体系中并不存在。丰田和本田首先明确市场可接受的价格，然后在此基础上倒推出厂价，把成本逐步分解，逐级降低。它们很清楚供应的成本水平、能否盈利等状况；对于供应的价格不达标但信誉好的供应商，丰田和本田会制定价格调整规划，放宽达标期限（如三年内），甚至适当降价。供应商们也愿意配合丰田和本田实现其定价目标。

在与供应商合作开发技术方面，丰田创建了客户工程师项目，即允许供应商选派自己的工程师到丰田的工厂与其工程师共事两三年,通过广泛的培训将供应商的业务全面整合到制造商的流程中，并形成自己的创意设计。这种合作经历提高了供应商的技术水平，也增加了它们对丰田的价值。丰田似乎不担心供应商的工程师们离开后的知识产权问题，因为丰田认为其供应商关系举措是市场上无法复制的竞争优势。

本田也经常选派自己的工程师（有时是高管）到供应商的工厂学习其运营和文化。本田通过广泛的测评系统不断考察供应商的质量、交货与事故状况，定期与供应商沟通，一旦出现问题，本田的高管将出面及时解决。本田对供应商绩效的密切关注保障了其供应商关系上的长期投资，也有助于供应商向行业标杆学习，进而不断培养供应商的能力。

通过帮助供应商在满足精确标准的过程中完善自己，丰田和本田建立了与供应商互惠互利的关系，使之能兵不血刃地从供应商处得到自己所需。

Hint for analysis and Reference answer

1. What are the drawbacks of developing deep supplier relationships of a company with its suppliers?

The drawback of developing deep supplier relationships of a company with its suppliers lies in that the decision of changing suppliers must be cautious since a company has spent a lot money and energy on existing suppliers. Once the cooperation is broken up, the transferring cost and risks incurred will increase.

2. What is Toyota's philosophy on working with suppliers?

Toyota's philosophy on working with suppliers is continuous improvement and respect to people. In building the relationships with suppliers, Toyota is demanding but adheres to a logical sequence. In negotiating with its suppliers, the Toyota personnel always respect the truth and seek fair deals rather than behind-screen transactions.

3. What qualities does Toyota look for in existing and potential suppliers?

The suppliers Toyota is looking for should be capable of manufacturing quality products with new technology and have cost advantage. Besides, suppliers must appoint a senior executive to lead the cooperation with Toyota.

4. What advice would you offer to the senior executives of procurement in building long-term supplier relationships?

A company's senior procurement executive should be really interested in the manufacturing session of its supplier and focus on the long-term cooperation in negotiating. "Putting yourself in others' shoes", seeking suppliers' respect and ensuing reward are always needed.

Case 2

Chemstar and Loftech

Chemstar Inc. manufactures and distributes chemicals at a plant and onsite distribution center in the western suburbs of Atlanta. Chemstar's purchasing manager is currently rethinking the firm's relationship with Loftech, Inc., a major supplier. Loftech has frequently delivered late, delivered the wrong order, or backordered Chemstar's supplies. Historically, Chemstar has dealt with supply problems by simply changing suppliers. The purchasing manager thinks that it may be time to consider additional changes.

Loftech is one of Chemstar's main suppliers. Loftech holds a large inventory, but some **slow- moving items**[1] must be ordered from Canada with up to three months' lead time. When Chemstar places an urgent order for these items, Loftech must order the items from Canada. Chemstar pressures Loftech about the slow delivery time, so Loftech appears to let Chemstar upset repeatedly.

Loftech's management wonders whether the business with Chemstar is worth keeping. Chemstar is a major client, but the constant threat of losing their business disrupts Loftech's operations. Top management may change the customer base to one that focuses on long-term customers and relies less on Chemstar.

The current process works like this. At the beginning of each month, Chemstar' customers estimate their requirements for the next month. Throughout the month they phone their orders to Chemstar' marketing department. Representatives from the marketing department relay the forecasts to the logistics department. Chemstar' purchasing department then orders from suppliers like Loftech. Chemstar's customers often place **expedited orders**[2], which cannot always be met because the stock is already reserved for other customers.

Questions for discussion

1. What are Chemstar's logistical problems?
2. How can Chemstar improve its logistical operations?
3. What should Loftech expect from its customers?
4. What options are available to Loftech in the short-term and the long-term?

New specialized terms

1. slow-moving item　滞销品
2. expedited order　加急订单

Case summary

Chemstar and Loftech

Chemstar 是一家化工产品制造与经销商，其工厂与现货配送中心均位于亚特兰大西郊。Chemstar 的主要供应商——Loftech 公司经常延迟交货、发错货或者延期供货，Chemstar 的采购经理正在重新思考与 Loftech 的关系问题。Chemstar 以往处理供应问题的做法就是更换供应商，这次采购经理认为，也许该做一些另外的改变了。

作为 Chemstar 主要供应商之一的 Loftech 持有大量库存，但一些慢销品必须从加拿大订货，备货期高达三个月。当 Chemstar 急需这些物品时，Loftech 再从加拿大采购，延误交货不可避免。Loftech 也因此屡屡令 Chemstar 失望。

Loftech 的管理层在犹豫是否继续与 Chemstar 做业务。诚然，Chemstar 是个主要客户，但其经常以"中断业务"相威胁而破坏 Loftech 的日常运作。Loftech 的高管或许会调整客户群，专注于那些注重长期客户关系的伙伴，减少对 Chemstar 的依赖。

当前的业务流程是这样的：每个月的月初 Chemstar 的客户估计他们下个月的需求，本月内他们都会通过电话向 Chemstar 的营销部门下订单，营销部的代表把预测的需求传递给物流部门，Chemstar 的采购部再从 Loftech 等供应商订货。Chemstar 的顾客经常发出紧急订单，这些订单不可能每次都及时交付，因为存货早已预留给了其他顾客。

Hint for analysis and Reference answer

1. What are Chemstar's logistical problems?

There exist two types of logistical problems: one is inbound logistics, another is outbound logistics. You can clearly understand the logistical problems through drawing an integrated logistics model.

2. How can Chemstar improve its logistical operations?

Chemstar can improve its logistical operations by taking the following measures:

(1) Joint planning with Loftech;

(2) Information sharing (communication) with both suppliers and customers;

(3) Sending in-time demand information to Loftech.

3. What should Loftech expect from its customers?

(1) More understanding, less complaining and threat of cutting off relations or change suppliers;

(2) less pressure about late delivery, etc.;

(3) Less urgent order, more planned order;

(4) Effective information exchange.

4. What options are available to Loftech in the short-term and the long-term?

The short-term option:

(1) Shorten the lead time of slow-moving items (ordered from Canada) by optimizing transportation network (considering combined transportation like ship-truck or ship-rail, etc.);

(2) Strengthen the communication with Chemstar's purchasers, let them know your plans, procedures of preparing goods and existing problems in advance.

The long-term option:

Establish sound relationship with both its customers and suppliers (from Canada) through joint effort. The key philosophy is forging strategic alliance with partners through joint planning, systematic operational information exchange, and corporate culture bridge building.

Case 3

FBK Industries: Supporting the Paradigm Shift in Vendor Selection through the Use of Multicriteria Methods for Sole-Sourcing

In today's business environment, Multiple Criteria Decision Making (MCDM) must be considered in procurement and other supply chain decisions. Whether brought about by quality considerations, the need to move toward JIT processing, or some other motivation, more complexity is necessarily involved in selecting vendors. The approaches suggested here — the SMART and DEA — should provide a good start toward facilitating multicriteria analyses in procurement.

Consider FBK Industries (FBK), a firm looking for a supplier to act as one of two sole-source vendors for a commodity group from which the firm consumes random quantities of between 10,000 and 20,000 units per month, depending upon demand. One vendor will be contracted for two years' worth of supply for half the items in the commodity group, while the other vendor will be contracted for the other half. Either vendor will serve as an alternate for the other should the latter not be able to meet FBK's needs. This is a commonly used procedure to minimize risk by maintaining good relations with alternate sources of supply in sole-source environments.

At present ten potential suppliers have been identified, all with strong reputations in at least one area. FBK has identified the five rights as fundamental criteria for selecting vendors. In addition, the firm has determined that it is important for supplier firms to be advanced with their information technology in order that ordering, billing, tracking, etc. might be streamlined. FBK also considers service and responsiveness a necessary criterion for its vendors, so that must also be incorporated into the decision. Hence, seven criteria are to be used in selecting a vendor.

Based upon past dealings with these ten firms, as well as reliable documentation from those firms, FBK has calculated the average price per unit for items in the commodity group for each of the vendors. FBK has also examined responsiveness of those firms and has noted the typical lead time for each. No particular objective measures were available for evaluating the firms according to the other criteria, but subjective evaluation is possible based upon the documentation provided by the firms. As a result, the procurement manager has been able to study the documentation and rate each firm according to a **seven-point Likert-type scale**[1] on each of the subjective criteria. More typically this type of subjective evaluation would be the result of the work of a cross-enterprise commodity team. In such cases, each member of the team would perform the subjective rating task and the evaluations of each member would be averaged for each criterion. These averages would then be used in place of the manager's assessments. Either way, a set of raw scores could be assembled for each of the vendors being considered.

Table1-1 summarizes the raw score data for the ten firms being considered for the **sole-sourcing contract**[2]. Values indicated for price are given as average cost per unit for the items being considered. For lead time, the values given are in days. Thus, for both price and lead time, small data values are preferable. The subjective ratings for the other criteria are such that a value of 7 indicates the best performance that might be expected and a value of 1 indicates the worst conceivable performance. Note that each vendor other than Vendor 2 is "best" at something; e.g., Vendor 1 has the best quality (tied with Vendors 5 and 6), while Vendor 3 rates best with respect to its ability to deliver directly to the right place, Vendor 7 has the best price, Vendor 6 has the best lead time, and so forth.

Table 1-1 Vendor Data for FBK Industries

Vendor	Price/$	Quality	Lead time	Quantity	Delivery	Tech	Service
1	8.75	7	3	6	6	3	5
2	7.25	2	2	4	4	4	4
3	10.24	6	4	2	7	3	4
4	11.28	6	2	1	6	7	5
5	11.20	7	2	4	3	7	6
6	11.73	7	1	4	6	4	7
7	6.00	3	4	5	4	5	4
8	9.77	5	2	7	1	5	6
9	11.10	6	3	3	2	7	4
10	8.91	5	3	7	7	4	6

One approach to selecting a supplier would be to determine ranks for the scores, average the ranks, and then choose the vendor with the best average. Such an approach makes it possible to combine data values involving different units of measure (e.g., points versus dollars), differing scales (e.g., from 6 to 11 versus 1 to 7), and inverse value assessments (e.g., less is better — price — versus more is better — quality). Averaging has two major flaws, however. First, it implicitly assigns equal importance to all criteria. Secondly, averaging assumes linear value functions within each criterion. Typically more (or less) of something is better but at a decreasing rate, yet linear value functions treat performance as if there is no declining benefit as ideals are approached. Hence, it seems appropriate to opt for multicriteria approaches that allow for the assignment of appropriate weights to the criteria and the incorporation of nonlinear value functions.

Numerous multicriteria (i.e., multiattribute) decision support tools have been developed for structuring and supporting such decisions. One popular procedure that incorporates such features is the simple **multiattribute rating technique**[3], or SMART, which determines additive multiattribute value scores for finite sets of alternatives. In short, SMART involves determining the criteria of importance, developing weights for those criteria, assessing the courses of action involved, scoring those alternatives according to the criteria, and synthesizing this information into a set of multicriteria scores, one for each of the alternatives being considered. Hence the multicriteria score for alternative j would have the value

$$z_j = \sum_i w_i s_{ij} \qquad (1)$$

where the w_i represent criterion weights and the s_{ij} represent the individual alternative scores for each of the criteria.

Many elementary discussions of purchasing principles address the "Five Rights" of purchasing. These are actually five criteria to be considered in procurement decisions and form the basis for the vendor selection problem. The criteria or "rights" are: the right price, the right place, the right timing, the right quality, and the right quantity. Good quality is important in that less safety stock is required, fewer repairs will be needed, warranty costs will be reduced, downstream processes function better, and overall product/service demand will be improved. Quantity and timing are particularly to JIT firms, where small quantities and short lead times are absolute necessities for maintaining the flows of goods in systems that require minimal inventories. Similarly, it is important that suppliers be capable of delivery directly to points of use rather than to intermediaries in order to reduce **non-value adding steps**[4]. Of course, obtaining the best price for procured goods and services is important, but, as indicated in Deming's fourth Point, initial price is not sufficient in itself as a basis for purchase. It is even argued by some that the least important of the five rights is price.

Stimson (2002) indicated that firms involved in vendor selection should consider, in addition to the five rights, possibly another five or so criteria. These are: the supplier's service/responsiveness; the supplier's technology and level of innovation; the supplier's operational compatibility with the customer firm; the strategic fit with the customer and supplier firms; the customer firm's importance to the supplier; and the extent to which the supplier is globalized.

Criterion weights — the w_i values in model (1) — reflect how important the various criteria are, relative to one another. Typically, it is desired that the weights sum to 1.000 (or 100%) thus allowing the weights to be interpreted according to their proportional importance. Suppose also that FBK wishes to adhere to some criterion weight guidelines such as those used by Stimson. Such guidelines represent policy constraints commonly imposed by upper management or possibly external constituents. Adaptations of these guidelines are given in Table 1-2, which also summarizes the remainder of the weight assessment procedure. If these guidelines are followed, then (contrary to what some might recommend) price would be considered among the most important two criteria, although the decision-maker (DM) in this case has ranked it somewhat less important than quality. Next in importance for FBK is lead time, followed by quantity, delivery, technology, and service.

In contrast to the SMART and other multicriteria selection tools, Data Envelopment Analysis (DEA) is a procedure not intended as a technique for choosing among alternatives. Instead, DEA was meant to evaluate the results of decision making and to identify a set **Pareto efficient outcomes**[5] from among a potentially large set of candidates. Bear in mind, nevertheless, that the decision-making process inherently involves evaluation, often explicitly, of the alternatives prior to selection. In the vendor selection problem, the alternatives can be (and essentially are) evaluated as if they were results. DEA might therefore be useful, especially if some modifications (enhancements actually) are made to the basic procedure.

Table 1-2 Weights for FBK Vendor Selection Criteria

	Min	Max	Points	Weight
Quality	0.200	0.350	100	0.267
Price	0.200	0.350	80	0.213
Lead time	0.100	0.200	60	0.160
Quantity	0.100	0.200	50	0.133
Service	0.100	0.200	40	0.107
Delivery	0.050	0.100	25	0.067
Technology	0.050	0.100	20	0.053

Data envelopment analysis was developed by Rhodes and initially detailed and publicized by Charnes et al (1978) for evaluating more than two decision outcomes and/or decision-making units (DMUs) with respect to their relative efficiencies, based upon multiple criteria. It was built on the theoretical foundations provided by Farrell and continues to be popular for a wide variety of applications. Beyond identifying efficient outcomes, DEA can be, and has been, used to identify the existence of technical and/or managerial efficiencies.

One version variation of DEA evaluates DMUs strictly on the basis of their process outputs, essentially the z_j values in model (1). For each DMU a set of criterion weights is determined so as to make that DMU's multiattribute value (MAV) score (z_j) look as good as possible when all other DMUs' scores are evaluated with the same set of weights. This could be done via some trial and error process to see the effects of various weighting schemes; however, DEA uses **linear programming (LP)**[6] to arrive more directly at the best set of weights for each DMU. The criterion weights comprise the decision variables, and the objective function is the MAV score for DMU being evaluated. There is a constraint for each DMU, restricting its MAV score to be no more than 1.000, the value defining maximum utility (as discussed above). Finally, all weights are required to be nonnegative, which reflects the assumption that more of an output is better. For each DMU under consideration (call it DMU_k) the resulting linear program, summarized in model (2), is formulated and then solved.

Maximize: $z_k = \sum_i w_i s_{ik}$

Subject to:

$$\sum_i w_i s_{ij} \leq 1.000 \; \forall \; j \qquad (2)$$

$$w_i \geq 0.000 \; \forall \; i$$

The overall process of evaluating all of the DMUs involves the solution of one model for each of the DMUs. Ordinarily there is no need to normalize the weights so they sum to 1.000 (or any other arbitrary value). There is also no need to express or convert the s_{ij} values so they reflect the same scale. Both of these procedures are obviated as the optimization process develops criterion weights accordingly; the weights would however be interpreted differently than they are in more typical multicriteria applications.

Note that the maximum possible value for z_k, as restricted by the first constraint set, is 1.000. If the value of the objective function at optimality equals 1.000, then DMU_k is said to be efficient. In such a circumstance, no other DMU has performed better with respect to all criteria than did DMU_k. On the other hand, if z_k is less than 1.000 at optimality, then DMU_k cannot be considered efficient. In other words, there is no weighting scheme that could cause the value of z_k for DMU_k to be as high as 1.000. When this occurs, the optimal value of z_k reflects how close DMU_k is to the efficient frontier. Solving model (2) for each of the DMUs reveals the set of nonefficient DMUs, as well as the (Pareto) efficient set of DMUs — those for which the optimal value of z_k is equal to 1.000. This latter group thus forms an empirically derived estimate of the efficient frontier for this problem, and the nonefficient DMUs can be ranked based upon how close they are to the efficient frontier.

At least one, and as many as all, constraints will be binding for any solution to model (2). If a constraint is binding at optimality, that means that the DMU corresponding to that constraint, would also be considered efficient based upon the weights determined by the optimization. Those DMUs for which corresponding constraints are binding is referred to as the reference set for a given nonefficient DMU_k, since they are the efficient DMUs with characteristics most closely resembling those of DMU_k.

In the vendor selection problem, the values in Table 1-1 would comprise the s_{ij} values in model (2). For example, without any modifications to the general DEA formulation, the first constraint would be

$$8.75w_1 + 7w_2 + 3w_3 + 6w_4 + 6w_5 + 3w_6 + 5w_7 \leqslant 1.000$$

Data envelopment analysis should thus reveal the best set of criterion weights for each vendor under consideration, as well as a reference set of similar vendors. However, the purpose of vendor selection is not to determine weights but to identify the best vendor. Only in rare circumstances will standard DEA result in a single efficient vendor and consequently provide a clear choice for the sole-sourcing decision. Furthermore, it makes little sense to allow the model to determine criterion weights, which are intended to reflect DM priorities and not characteristics of the data. Identifying an efficient set of vendors out of a relatively large group may have some value, but modifications are nevertheless called for in order for DEA to have true relevance to the vendor selection problem.

Recall that guidelines have been suggested for weights for the various criteria and that those guidelines are summarized in Table 1-2. Such guidelines could be expressed as a set of constraints added to model (2), and the modified linear program is that summarized in model (3):

Maximize: $z_k = \sum_i w_i s_{ik}$

Subject to:

$$\sum_i w_i s_{ij} \leqslant 1.000 \ \forall \ j \tag{3}$$

$$w_i \geqslant L_i \sum_i w_i \ \forall \ i$$

$$w_i \leqslant U_i \sum_i w_i \ \forall \ i$$

$$w_i \geqslant 0.000 \ \forall \ i$$

The additional constraints simply indicate that any given weight w_i must be no less than a specified minimum proportion (L_i) of the criterion weight sum and no more than a specified maximum proportion (U_i) of that sum. For example, for the timing (i.e., lead time) criterion, the values of L_i and U_i would be 0.100 and 0.200, respectively, as indicated in Table 1-2.

The incorporation of the criterion weight constraints, however, requires the vendor scores (the s_{ij} values) for each of the criteria to be consistent in scale. That is, a very good result (or score) should be close to 1.000 for any of the criteria and a bad result close to 0.000 if a scale of 0 through 1 is being used to score the vendors. Otherwise a criterion might receive undue weight (importance) simply by virtue of the scale of the scores on that criterion. This poses little trouble and, in fact, provides an opportunity to incorporate value scores that are nonlinear. The DEA procedure treats all data values as corresponding to linear value scales unless some sort of transformation takes place with the raw data. As with the SMART, the decision-maker can assign a value between 0.000 and 1.000 to each of the s_{ij} values in model (3) based upon the desirability of the results on the criteria involved. For example, based upon the simulated DM scores (s values) in Table 1-3, the first constraint in model (3) would be

$$0.87w_1 + 1.00w_2 + 0.86w_3 + 0.95w_4 + 0.95w_5 + 0.25w_6 + 0.75w_7 \leqslant 1.000$$

rather than

$$8.75w_1 + 7w_2 + 3w_3 + 6w_4 + 6w_5 + 3w_6 + 5w_7 \leqslant 1.000$$

as in model (2). The first weight guideline constraint in model (3) would be

$$w_1 \geqslant 0.200 \, (w_1 + w_2 + w_3 + w_4 + w_5 + w_6 + w_7)$$

representing the quality criterion.

Table 1-3 Scoring of Vendors According to Criteria

Vendor	Price		Quality		Lead time		Quantity		Delivery		Technology		Service	
	x	s	x	s	x	s	x	s	x	s	x	s	x	s
1	8.75	0.87	7	1.00	3	0.86	6	0.95	6	0.95	3	0.25	5	0.75
2	7.25	0.92	2	0.05	2	0.92	4	0.50	4	0.50	4	0.50	4	0.50
3	10.24	0.79	6	0.95	4	0.78	2	0.05	7	1.00	3	0.25	4	0.50
4	11.28	0.71	6	0.95	2	0.92	1	0.00	6	0.95	7	1.00	5	0.75
5	11.20	0.72	7	1.00	2	0.92	4	0.50	3	0.25	7	1.00	6	0.95
6	11.73	0.66	7	1.00	1	0.95	4	0.50	6	0.95	4	0.50	7	1.00
7	6.00	0.95	3	0.25	4	0.78	5	0.75	4	0.50	5	0.75	4	0.50
8	9.77	0.82	5	0.75	2	0.92	7	1.00	1	0.00	5	0.75	6	0.95
9	11.10	0.73	6	0.95	3	0.86	3	0.25	2	0.05	7	1.00	4	0.50
10	8.91	0.87	5	0.75	3	0.86	7	1.00	7	1.00	4	0.50	6	0.95

In summary, just as with the SMART, applying DEA to the vendor selection begins with the identification of alternatives and the determination of the criteria to be used for evaluating the vendors. Rather than proceeding from there with the determination of criterion weights, however, DEA skips to the scoring the alternatives according to the criteria. The scoring would then be done in the same manner as in the SMART. Results of the scoring in turn become the data used to instantiate the LP models (3), which are then solved, generating efficiency scores for each of the vendors. A DMU (or alternative) with an efficiency score of 1.000 should be considered for selection; if more than one DMU is efficient (i.e., has a score of 1.000), a means of breaking the tie is needed. One approach suggested in the literature for doing so is to select the efficient vendor that appears most in the reference groups of the nonefficient vendors.

Part One　Procurement and Supplier Management

Comparison of the Methods

Both multicriteria approaches identify Vendor 1 as the best, and selection of the top two vendors would be the same for either method. Rankings are generally the same or differing by one place across the multicriteria methods. Note, however, how substantial difference exists between the results of the averaging approach and the results of the multicriteria approaches. The averaging approach thus illustrates (as intended) the importance of using appropriate weights for the various criteria rather than simply aggregating the scores. Within the two multicriteria techniques, very little difference results, at least in this case (i.e., with these data). This should be expected, as they are based upon the same theoretical model, as given by model (1). Ultimately, however, comparisons should be made using a number of varying data sets to identify circumstances that might lead to favoring one or the other method.

▷ Questions for discussion

1. Which vendor(s) should FBK select according to SMART and DEA?
2. Identify what further information would be helpful for evaluating the candidates, as well as how that information might feasibly be obtained.
3. What are the limitations associated with using these MCDM approaches? How do the results of these approaches differ from each other, and what are the financial ramifications of using these MCDM approaches rather than a purely traditional price-based decision or an unweighted averaging approach across the multiple criteria?

▷ New specialized terms

1. seven-point Likert-type scale　李克特七级量表
2. sole-sourcing contract　独家供货合同
3. multiattribute rating technique　多属性评分方法
4. non-value adding step　非增值环节
5. Pareto efficient outcome　帕累托最优收益
6. linear programming (LP)　线性规划

Case summary

FBK Industries：通过独家采购的多标准方法，支持转变供应商选择范式

在当今的商业环境中，采购与其他供应链决策必须考虑多标准决策思路。出于质量把控、准时制处理或其他动机，供应商的选择日趋复杂。SMART法和数据包络分析（DEA）

是有利于采购中应用多标准分析的良好起点。FBK 公司正在两家独家供货商之中选择一家,作为其大宗商品供应商,以满足其每月 10 000 至 20 000 单位的需求。这两家供应商各供应一半商品,签约两年。如果其中某家无法满足 FBK 的需求,另一家就取而代之。目前已确定了十个备选的供应商,FBK 在选择供应商时将参照七项标准。

根据过去与这十家公司的交易以及这些公司的可靠文件,FBK 计算了每个供应商的商品组中每件商品的平均价格。FBK 还核定了这些公司的响应能力,并查证了每个公司通常的备货期。没有特别客观的措施可用于根据其他标准评估公司,但可以根据公司提供的单证进行主观评估。因此,采购经理能够根据每个主观标准上的李克特七级量表来研究单证并对每个公司进行评级。

表 1-1 总结了正在考虑签订独家供货合同的十家公司的原始得分数据。价格指示的值是所考虑项目的每单位平均成本。备货期的数值以天为单位。因此,对于价格和提前期,数值越小越好。其他标准的主观评级是,数值 7 表示可能预期的最佳表现,数值 1 表示最差的预期表现。请注意,供应商 2 以外的每个供应商都有表现"最佳"的特征。例如,供应商 1 具有最佳质量(与供应商 5 和 6 并列),而供应商 3 在直接交付到正确地点的能力方面评价最佳,供应商 7 具有最佳价格,供应商 6 具有最短的备货期,等等。

多属性决策支持工具可以构建和支持这样的决策,其中一种流行的方法是简单的多属性评级技术,即 SMART,它确定有限的替代方案的附加多属性值分数。SMART 涉及确定重要性的标准并为这些标准制定权重,评估所涉及的行动方案,根据标准对这些备选方案进行评分,并将这些信息综合成一组多准则分数,每个备选方案对应一个分数。因此,选项 j 的多准则得分将具有如下值:

$$z_j = \sum_i w_i s_{ij} \tag{1}$$

其中 w_i 表示标准权重,s_{ij} 表示每个标准的各个备选方案的分数。

许多涉及采购决策原则的讨论都认为选择供应商的基本标准是五个"适当",即适当的价格,适当的渠道(地点),适当的时间,适当的质量和适当的数量。Stimson(2002)指出,除了这五个"适当"之外,还应包括另外五个标准:供应商的响应能力、供应商的技术与创新水平、供应商与客户的业务兼容性、供应商战略与客户战略的匹配性、供应商的全球化程度。

标准权重——模型(1)中的 w_i 值——反映了各种标准相对于彼此的重要程度。通常,期望权重总和为 1.000(或 100%),从而可以根据权重比例判断其重要性。还假设 FBK 希望遵守一些标准权重指南,如 Stimson 使用的标准权重指南。这些指导方针代表了高层管理人员或外部成员通常施加的政策限制。表 1-2 给出了这些准则的选编指标,还总结了权重评估程序的其余项目。如果遵循这些指导原则,那么(与某些人可能推荐的相反)价格将被认为是最重要的两个标准之一,尽管在这种情况下决策者对价格的排名不如质量重要。接下来,FBK 的重要性是备货期,其次是数量、服务、交货和技术。

与 SMART 和其他多标准选择工具相比,数据包络分析(DEA)是一类程序,但并不是一种用于选择替代方案的技术,其目的在于评估决策结果,并从潜在的一大批候选方案中确定一组能达到帕累托最优收益的供应商,但决策制定过程的本质是在选择之前对替代方案进行明确的评估。事实上,在供应商选择问题中,备选方案可以(并且基本上)被当作选定的结果进行评估。因此,特别是在如果对基本程序进行一些修改(实际上是增强),DEA 可能是有用的。

数据包络分析主要用于根据多个标准评估两个以上的决策结果和/或决策单元(DMU)的相对效率。除了确定有效的结果之外,DEA 可以并且一直用于确定技术和/或管理效率的存在。

DEA 的一个变体严格地根据其过程输出来评估 DMU,基本上是模型(1)中的 z_j 值。对于每个 DMU,确定一组标准权重,以便当使用相同的权重集评估所有其他 DMU 的分数时,使得 DMU 的多属性值分数(z_j)看起来尽可能好。这可以通过一些试错过程来完成,以了解各种加权方案的效果。然而,DEA 使用线性规划(LP)更直接地到达每个 DMU 的最佳权重集。标准权重包括决策变量,目标函数是被评估的 DMU 的 MAV 分数。每个 DMU 都有一个约束,限制其 MAV 分数不超过 1.000,该值定义最大效用。最后,所有权重都必须是非负的,这反映了"输出结果越多越好"的假设。对于所考虑的每个 DMU(称之为 DMU_k),可以推导出其线性规划表达式,见模型(2),然后求解得出可行方案。

目标函数(最大值): $z_k = \sum_i w_i s_{ik}$

约束条件:

$$\sum_i w_i s_{ij} \leqslant 1.000 \ \forall \ j \tag{2}$$

$$w_i \geqslant 0.000 \ \forall \ i$$

评估所有 DMU 的整个过程涉及每个 DMU 模型的解决方案。通常不需要对权重进行标准化,以便使它们总和为 1.000(或任何其他任意值),也没有必要标示或转换 s_{ij} 值,以便使它们反映相同的比例。由于优化过程相应地开发了标准权重,因此避免了这两个过程。然而,权重的解释与在更典型的多准则应用中的权重不同。

请注意,受第一个约束集限制的 z_k 的最大可能值为 1.000。如果目标函数的最优值等于 1.000,则说明 DMU_k 是有效的。在这种情况下,没有其他 DMU 在所有标准方面表现优于 DMU_k。另外,如果 z_k 在最佳状态下小于 1.000,则不能认为 DMU_k 是有效的。换句话说,没有加权方案可能导致 DMU_k 的 z_k 值高达 1.000。当发生这种情况时,z_k 的最佳值反映了 DMU_k 与有效边界的接近程度。求解每个 DMU 的模型(2)揭示了一组无效的 DMU,以及帕累托有效的 DMU 集合——那些 z_k 的最佳值等于 1.000 的 DMU。后一组因此形成了针对该问题的有效边界的经验导出的估计值,并且可以基于它们与有效边界的接近程度来对非高效 DMU 进行排序。

对于模型(2)的任何解决方案,至少一个约束条件将具有约束力。如果约束在最优状态下绑定,则意味着对应于该约束的 DMU 也将基于由优化确定的权重而被认为是有效的。对于有约束力的那些 DMU 被称为给定无效 DMU_k 的参考集,因为它们是具有与 DMU_k 最接近特征的有效 DMU。

在供应商选择问题中,表 1-1 中的值将包括模型(2)中的 s_{ij} 值。例如,在不对一般 DEA 公式进行任何修改的情况下,第一个约束是:

$$8.75w_1 + 7w_2 + 3w_3 + 6w_4 + 6w_5 + 3w_6 + 5w_7 \leq 1.000$$

因此,数据包络分析应揭示所考虑的每个供应商的最佳标准权重集,以及类似供应商的参考集。但是,供应商选择的目的不是确定权重,而是确定最佳供应商。只有在极少数情况下,标准 DEA 才会产生一个有效的供应商,从而为单一采购决策提供明确的选择。此外,允许模型确定标准权重是没有意义的,标准权重旨在反映 DM 优先级而不是数据的特征。从相对较大的组中识别出一组有效的供应商才具有一定的价值,但是仍需要进行修改以使 DEA 与供应商选择问题具有真正的相关性。

回顾一下那些建议作为各种标准权重的准则,以及表 1-2 中总结的那些准则。这些准则可以表述为一组约束条件附加到模型(2)中,修正后的线性规划表达式见模型(3):

目标函数:$z_k = \sum_i w_i s_{ik}$

约束条件:

$$\sum_i w_i s_{ij} \leq 1.000 \ \forall \ j \tag{3}$$

$$w_i \geq L_i \sum_i w_i \ \forall \ i$$

$$w_i \leq U_i \sum_i w_i \ \forall \ i$$

$$w_i \geq 0.000 \ \forall \ i$$

附加约束表明:任何给定权重 w_i 必须不小于标准权重和的指定最小比例(L_i)并且不超过该总和的指定最大比例(U_i)。例如,对于定时(即提前期)标准,那些 L_i 与 U_i 的值将分别为 0.100 和 0.200,如表 1-2 所示。

然而,纳入标准权重的约束条件要求每个标准的供应商得分(s_{ij} 值)在尺度上是一致的。也就是说,对于任何标准,如果使用 0 到 1 的等级来对供应商进行评分,非常好的结果(或得分)应接近 1.000,差的结果接近 0.000;否则,某个标准可能仅仅通过该标准上的尺度被赋予过大的权重(重要性)。这不会带来什么麻烦,事实上,它提供了一个纳入非线性赋值的机会。除非对原始数据进行某种转换,否则 DEA 过程将所有数据值视为对应于线性值标度。与 SMART 一样,决策者可以根据所涉及标准的结果的理想程度,为模型(3)中的每个 s_{ij} 值分配 0.000 和 1.000 之间的值。例如,基于表 1-3 中的模拟 DM 分数(s 值),模型(3)中的第一个约束是:

$$8.75w_1 + 7w_2 + 3w_3 + 6w_4 + 6w_5 + 3w_6 + 5w_7 \leq 1.000$$

而不是模型（2）中的约束：

$$8.75w_1 + 7w_2 + 3w_3 + 6w_4 + 6w_5 + 3w_6 + 5w_7 \leqslant 1.000$$

模型（3）中的第一个权重准则约束将是：

$$w_1 \geqslant 0.200\,(w_1 + w_2 + w_3 + w_4 + w_5 + w_6 + w_7)$$

总之，与 SMART 一样，将 DEA 应用于供应商选择，首先要确定备选方案，并确定用于评估供应商的标准。然而，DEA 不是从起始点继续确定标准权重，而是跳转到根据标准对备选方案进行评分，然后以与 SMART 中相同的方式完成评分。评分结果反过来成为用于实证线性规划模型的数据，然后求解这些模型，从而为每个供应商生成效率分数。应考虑选择效率得分为 1.000 的 DMU（或替代）；如果多于一个 DMU 是有效的（即得分为 1.000），则需要打破平局的手段。文献中提出的一种方法是选择在高效供应商的参考组中出现最多的有效供应商。

两种多标准方法都将供应商 1 标识为最佳，且排名前两位的供应商的选择对于任一种方法都是相同的。但需注意的是，平均方法的结果与多标准方法的结果之间存在显著差异。因此，平均方法说明了对各种标准使用适当权重的重要性，而不是简单地汇总分数。在两种多标准技术中，至少在这个案例中（即使用这些数据）产生非常小的差异。这应该是可以预期的，因为它们基于相同的理论模型，如模型（1）所给出的。但是，最终应使用许多不同的数据集进行比较，以识别可能导致偏好一种或另一种方法的情形。

▶ Hint for analysis and Reference answer

1. Which vendor(s) should FBK select according to SMART and DEA?

According to the SMART procedure, Vendors 1 and 10 are the first and second choice, respectively. The DEA results show that Vendors 1 and 10 are both efficient. Vendor 1 serves as the only member of reference sets for six of the nonefficient vendors, while Vendor 10 is sole member in the reference sets for only two nonefficient vendors. Consequently, both vendors would receive sole-source contracts, and Vendor 1 would receive preferential treatment. The results are summarized in Table1-4 (For comparison purposes, the rankings of the vendors are shown also according to simple rank averaging approach).

2. Identify what further information would be helpful for evaluating the candidates, as well as how that information might feasibly be obtained.

Further information that would be helpful include the supplier's operational compatibility with the customer firm; the strategic fit with the customer and supplier firms; the customer firm's importance to the supplier; and the extent to which the supplier is globalized.

Such information might be obtained from FBK's market research or shared with partners through ERP, CRM, or other SCM techniques.

表 1-4　根据 DEA 计算的 FBK 的供应商选择结果 Selection

供应商	DEA 效率	Reference 赋值	Ranks DEA	SMART	平均值
1	1.000	n/a	1	1	4
2	0.670	10	10	10	7
3	0.802	1	8	7	10
4	0.880	1	6	6	6
5	0.955	1	5	4	1
6	0.959	1	4	3	1
7	0.757	10	9	9	8
8	0.970	1	3	5	5
9	0.815	1	7	8	9
10	1.000	n/a	1	2	1

3. What are the limitations associated with using these MCDM approaches? How do the results of these approaches differ from each other, and what are the financial implications of using these MCDM approaches rather than a purely traditional price-based decision or an unweighted averaging approach across the multiple criteria?

One limitation is that the one-time contract (e.g., bidder selection) problem is not addressed here. Second, a comparison study of how these MCDM approaches will rank vendors under a variety of differing circumstances is not undertaken. Furthermore, the decision environment in this case is rather simple, therefore, a means of incorporating complexity should be explored.

SMART involves determining the criteria of importance, developing weights for those criteria, assessing the courses of action involved, scoring those alternatives according to the criteria, and synthesizing this information into a set of multicriteria scores, one for each of the alternatives being considered. In contrast to SMART, DEA is a procedure not intended as a technique for choosing among alternatives. Instead, DEA was meant to evaluate the results of decision making and to identify a set Pareto efficient outcomes from among a potentially large set of candidates.

Financial Implications: FBK is making a decision concerning the annual purchase of approximately 180,000 units which could cost as little as $6.00 each on average. That means an annual cost of approximately $1,080,000 if Vendor 7 were chosen. However, that vendor is ranked ninth overall according to either of the multicriteria techniques. Awarding the sole source contracts to the top two vendors per the multicriteria approaches would, on the other hand, result in an estimated average annual cost of $1,589,400. That is, 180,000 units would be purchased, half at $8.75 (Vendor 1) and the other half at $8.91 (Vendor 2). This means the premium FBK would be paying to pursue objectives beyond cost minimization is over $500,000 or 50%. There must consequently be at least an equivalent offsetting benefit to the firm in order for this to be justified, especially given the leverage involved. Since much of the benefit from improved purchasing is likely to be intangible, a monumental task may be involved in convincing top management and shareholders of the validity of multicriteria approaches to vendor selection.

Part Two

Logistics Marketing Management

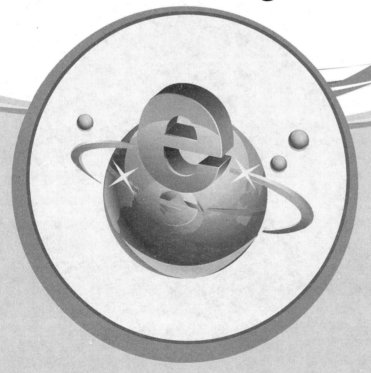

Part Two Logistics Marketing Management

Learning Objectives

After learning this part, you will be able to:
- Explain the process of logistics marketing management
- Gain an understanding of handling channel conflicts and customer complaints
- Get an overview of service marketing mix
- Understand the importance of employee satisfaction in logistics firms

Case 4

UPS and FedEx turn focus to consumer behavior

On the ground floor of United Parcel Service's $2.2bn Worldport Hub, workers are stunting into huge **airfreight containers**[1] some of the roughly 1.1 million packages that the center in Louisville, Kentucky, handles every night.

Most of the containers have sped through Worldport's maze of whirring conveyor belts and been reloaded in less than four hours. At 2:30 am, some of the 100 or so flights that will carry the packages around the US and the world are starting to leave.

Amid the dazzling efficiency, however, is evidence of the significant challenge that UPS and FedEx, its main US rival, are facing. Many of the boxes bear the logo of Zappos. com, the internet footwear retailer. Another box contains frozen artificial skin for use in surgery, while one bears the simple legend, "Live Tropical Fish".

Online retailing and **business-to-business ordering**[2] are driving up traffic volumes for both UPS and FedEx but also making flows harder to predict.

The question for both companies is whether management changes and technology investments can help them to avoid a repeat of the chaos that engulfed UPS last Christmas, when demand surged more than anticipated. Volumes on its busiest day, December 23, were 13 percent up on 2012's peak and the network was clogged. Many packages were delivered after December 25.

The problems reflect the behavior of the individual consumers who increasingly drive big operators' deliveries worldwide, according to Alan Braithwaite, a UK-based logistics consultant. They are more likely than logistics operators' **corporate customers**[3] to order at the last minute.

"The peaks are getting even peakier," he says.

Fewer goods are being delivered in bulk via single stops on vehicles routes to retail outlets, according to Henry Maier, chief executive of FedEx Ground, the company's road-delivery division.

"Now those individual items get boxed up and sent to somebody's house, so that creates a stop," Mr. Maier says, "The challenge across the industry is managing the stops."

UPS is improving its management systems and investing $500 million in extra capital spending this year to boost capacity, according to Kurt Kuehn, the group's **chief financial officer**[4].

"We're very focused on expanding capabilities and capacity to meet the current growth, not to mention the peak season," Mr. Kuehn says, "We have what is in many ways an enviable problem."

One of UPS's efficiency-boosting investments is on display at the Louisville Centennial Hub, a base for UPS's ground operations near Worldport. Jerry Durham, a driver, each morning consults a bank of computers running Orion, a new computer system, to work out the most efficient route between his scheduled **drop-offs**[5].

The technology has raised the average number of drop-offs per mile from 1.9 when drivers devised their own routes to 2.2 now, says Roger Hicks, UPS's business manager for Louisville East.

The system has overcome his initial skepticism, according to Mr. Durham. "I've gotten to like it a lot more," he says. Mr. Maier praises new hand-held scanners for boosting FedEx's efficiency. The scanners know the GPS coordinates of every address in the US and will alert drivers if they appear to be delivering in the wrong place. Such technology helps to cut down worker errors, especially among temporary staff taken on for the peak season.

"It makes our temporary resources much more effective," Mr. Maier says.

An innovation at Centennial typifies UPS's approach. In the past year, sorters have been given technology that scans package labels and tells them into which delivery bag they should post them. The technology has cut down on wasteful "mis-sorts".

Mr. Kuehn says most investments are focused on such local hubs, rather than the efficient Worldport, and predominantly into computer systems.

Yet, for UPS, last Christmas's biggest failing may have been in communication rather than in technology. UPS failed to spot its customers' higher than expected order volumes in time. Much of the short-term effort has focused on ensuring future volume forecasts and communications with customers are better than last year's. FedEx says that such forecasting also plays a key role in its peak-season planning.

"We're working with some large customers to get enhanced visibility," Mr. Kuehn says.

In the long run, meanwhile both companies expect to overcome the challenges partly through making more of their facilities like Worldport.

FedEx already operates all 33 of its ground network's hubs in the US on Worldport's highly automated model, with minimal handling by humans. Mr. Maier says it expects to start introducing such advanced technology in still more, smaller facilities.

For UPS, meanwhile, Worldport, the world's biggest **fully automated package-handling facility**[6], remains noticeably more advanced than smaller hubs such as Centennial, where much sorting is still by hand.

As the company adapts to the challenges of handling more shoes, medical supplies and fish, that will have to change, Mr. Kuehn says.

"Worldport is a highly automated, incredible asset, driven by technology," he says. "There are several other generations of buildings around the country that we're going to be renovating to look more like Louisville."

Customized needs

In the middle of a warehouse near the end of Louisville Airport's runway stands a line of **heavy-duty freezers**[7], an electronic stopwatch sitting on the lid of one. The stopwatch is intended to protect the delicate sheets of artificially-grown skin inside the freezers, used to treat diabetics' foot ulcers. Supervisors time how long each freezer is open when stocks are being retrieved, to ensure the temperature stays low enough.

The business in the warehouse illustrates how thoroughly UPS and other logistics companies have involved themselves in some customers' operations. Next to the skin freezers, workers are preparing to ship batches of influenza vaccine. In another section of the building, workers are putting together packages of mobile telephones for Sprint, the mobile telecoms company. They customize devices for customers with special requirements, including government departments that want employees' phone cameras disabled.

Such supply chain business is separate from the flagship express parcel operations of UPS, FedEx and other logistics operators but adds a vital extra dimension to the services they can offer companies. According to Rich Shaver, division manager for healthcare in UPS's Americas Central District, the growing popularity of outsourcing reflects the increasing pressure on healthcare companies to save money and compete more effectively.

"The customers have to have a competitive advantage," he says. "The only way they can have competitive advantage is if they have a very nimble, **flexible supply chain**[8] that at the same time is looking for what regulations and changes are coming."

The healthcare business, unlike high technology, remains relatively conservative and goods are shipped mostly to retail outlets, hospitals and other corporate customers.

However, the Louisville warehouse already employs pharmacists to handle prescriptions for some goods heading direct to customers. The company is receiving increasing numbers of requests to suggest ways that customers can deliver more healthcare products direct to consumers, according to Mr. Shaver.

"Most times, it's going to be a progressive, step-by-step process," he says.

▶ Questions for discussion

1. What issues are UPS and FedEX facing here?
2. How do UPS and FedEX contribute to their clients achieving a competitive advantage?
3. What are the drivers for collaboration in the examples given?

▶ New specialized terms

1. airfreight container   空运集装箱
2. business-to-business ordering   企业对企业（B2B）的订货
3. corporate customer   企业客户
4. chief financial officer   首席财务官
5. drop-off   快递（集货）点
6. fully automated package-handling facility   全自动包裹处理设施
7. heavy-duty freezer   重型冷藏车
8. flexible supply chain   敏捷供应链

Case summary

联合包裹服务公司（UPS）与联邦快递（FedEx）转向关注消费者行为

在联合包裹服务公司 22 亿美元的 Worldport 物流中心底层，在肯塔基州路易斯维尔市中心，每晚由工人分选处理约 110 万个包裹，装入大型空运集装箱。大多数集装箱快速通过 Worldport 迷宫般的旋转传送带，并在不到四小时内重新装载。这令人炫目的高效操作，也验证了 UPS 和其美国地区主要竞争对手——联邦快递正在面临的重大挑战。许多箱子带着鞋类电商"Zappos"的标识，有的箱子装着外科手术用的冷冻人造皮肤；有的箱子则标识着"活体热带鱼"的图案。

在线零售和 B2B（企业对企业）订购刺激着 UPS 和联邦快递提升其货运量，也使得货物流量更难以预测。两家公司共同面临的问题是，管理层的变革和技术投资是否可以帮助他们避免重复去年圣诞节 UPS 遭遇的混乱局面。当时需求大大超过预期，比 2012 年的峰值（最繁忙的是 12 月 23 日）激增了 13%，运输网络因此瘫痪，许多包裹被迫在 12 月 25 日之后交付。

英国物流顾问 Alan Braithwaite 表示，这些问题是个体消费者行为的结果，他们越来越多地把大型运营商的业务推向全球范围，且比物流运营商的企业客户更有可能在最后一刻下单。这位顾问说："需求的峰值越来越高。"据联邦快递公路运输部门首席执行官 Henry Maier 称，单一站点停靠、大批量运输的货物趋于减少，个人物品集结后再送往某人的住处，由此增加了一个停靠点。如何应对这些停靠点，是整个行业面临的最大挑战。

据该集团的首席财务官 Kurt Kuehn 称，UPS 正在改进其管理系统并将投入 5 亿美元提高运能。

Kuehn 先生说，他们十分注重扩大运能与满足当前增长的能力，更不用说是旺季了。UPS 为了提升效率的其中一个投资项目正在路易斯维尔百年纪念中心启动，该中心是 UPS 在 Worldport 附近的陆地运营基地。司机 Jerry Durham 每天早上都会从一套运行 Orion（一种新的计算机系统）的计算机上找到连接各个收货点之间的最有效的路线。路易斯维尔东部的 UPS 业务经理 Roger Hicks 表示，该技术将每英里平均到达 1.9 个收货点（由驾驶员设计自己路线）增加到了现在的 2.2 个。这套系统打消了 Durham 先生当初的顾虑，日益受到他的青睐。Maier 先生还赞扬了新的手持式扫描仪，这种扫描仪知道美国每个地址的 GPS 坐标，当出现可能送错货时，他们会提醒司机。这种技术有助于减少工人的错误，特别是在旺季招聘的临时工作人员。在过去的一年中，分拣员还掌握了通过扫描包装标签分类张贴的技术，如此大大减少了分拣失误带来的浪费。

然而，对于 UPS 来说，去年圣诞节失败的主要原因可能是沟通而不是技术。UPS 未能及时发现客户的订单量高于预期。所以，大部分短期内的工作都专注于确保满足预测的需求量，与客户的沟通也好于去年。联邦快递认为，此类预测在其旺季业务规划中也起着关键作用。Kuehn 先生说："我们正在与一些大客户合作，致力于提高业务的能见度。"

从长远来看，两家公司都希望部分地通过增加像 Worldport 这样的设施来克服挑战。

联邦快递已经在 Worldport 的高度自动化模式下运营其在美国的所有 33 个地面网络枢纽，将人工操作降到最低。同时，对于 UPS 而言，世界上最大的全自动包裹处理设施 Worldport 仍然比 Centennial 这样仍须大量手工分类的小型枢纽更为先进。在公司适应了如何处理鞋类产品的挑战之后，医疗物资与鱼类产品的操作也需要改变。Worldport 是技术推动的高度自动化的惊人资产，UPS 将要对散落在美国其他地方的若干旧楼房进行更新改造，使之更像路易斯维尔的设施。

在靠近路易斯维尔机场跑道末端的一座仓库中间，有一排重型冷藏车，其中一辆车顶放置了一块电子秒表，用于监控冷藏车内人造皮肤（用于治疗糖尿病引发的足溃疡）的温度。这类仓库业务表明，UPS 与其他物流公司已经融入了客户的业务运营中。皮肤冷藏车旁边，工人们在准备装运流感疫苗；在库房的另一处，工人们正在为 Sprint（移动电信公司）分装手机，Sprint 为那些有特定要求的客户定制设备，包括政府部门，他们要求员工配备不带拍照功能的手机。

UPS、FedEx 与其他物流运营商的这类供应链业务是独立于主打的快递包裹业务的，但能够增加其客户服务的内容。UPS 的美国中部保健部主管 Rich Shaver 认为，日益流行的外包反映了保健类公司所承受的精打细算、更有效开展竞争的压力。他说："客户必须具备竞争优势，而获取竞争优势的唯一途径是在面临各种规制与变化的形势时，能否打造一条精巧、敏捷的供应链。"不像高科技公司，保健类公司相对保守，产品多数运往零售店、医院与其他企业客户。然而，路易斯维尔的仓库已开始聘用药剂师处理一些直接面向客户的药品配方事宜了。Shaver 先生透露，他的公司收到越来越多的建议，要求客户将保健品直接送到消费者那里，这是个渐进的稳步发展的过程。

▶ Hint for analysis and Reference answer

1. What issues are UPS and FedEx facing here?

The tough issues challenging UPS and FedEx are booming online retailing and B2B ordering, repeat of chaos happened in peak seasons, diversified and dispersed consumer demand, and how to manage the constantly changing stops.

2. How do UPS and FedEx contribute to their clients achieving a competitive advantage?

They are making more of their facilities operate like Worldport (automation; heavy tech-intensive, etc.), deeply involved in customers' operation, working with customers to get enhanced visibility, and building a nimble flexible supply chain

3. What are the drivers for collaboration in the examples given?

Higher customers' expectation, growing popularity of outsourcing and new competition lying in supply chain integration are all drivers for collaboration in the examples given.

Case 5

Handy Tider, Inc.

Handy Tider, Inc., produced residential **trash compactors**[1] at a factory in St. Louis, Missouri, and sold them throughout the United States. Over 90 percent of Handy Tider's sales were in large urban areas where trash-collection costs were high.

The standard model compactor was about 3 feet high, 2 feet deep, and 1 1/3 feet wide, and the deluxe model had the same dimensions but contained better features such as greater capacity and greater horsepower. Because most of the compactors would be placed in home kitchens, a wide variety of colors and trims were manufactured, providing an exterior that would match many kitchen decors.

The standard model came in five colors with three different trims for a total of 15 different combinations, while the deluxe model came in eight colors and four different trims for a total of 32 different combinations. Retail prices were set by the dealer, with prices for the standard model ranging between $600 and $725 and for the deluxe model between $950 and $1,100. Sales in an area were usually slow until trash collectors, faced with rising **landfill costs**[2], raised their rates per can of refuse picked up.

There was one authorized Handy Tider **factory distributor**[3] in each large urban area and the distributor was responsible for filling orders from licensed Handy Tider retailers. The factory distributors were also allowed to sell compactors to the final consumers. Each factory distributor maintained a complete stock of all styles and trims of the Handy Tider compactors, and these distributors were required to stock at least five units of each of the 47 different styles available.

Because of the sporadic sales patterns and the wide number of colors and trims available, the **licensed retailers**[3] usually stocked only a display unit or two. Each retailer carried a "design your dream compactor" software package that allowed prospective buyers to design the model, color, and the trim they wanted. When the retailer completed the sale, the order would be transmitted to the nearest Handy Tider factory distributor.

The general agreement between the factory distributors and Handy Tider was that the distributors would deliver and install the compactor within five days after receiving an order from a licensed retailer. For the delivery and installation, the factory distributor received 9 percent of the unit's wholesale price, half paid by the licensed retailer that had made the sale and half paid by Handy Tider.

Bob Ortega worked in Handy Tider's distribution department in the St. Louis headquarters. He currently was working on a project to determine whether the compactor's **warranty**[5] should be extended from one year to two years. The units were well built, and there had been almost no warranty work requested in the first year of each model's life. Because Handy Tider would have no records of repair work performed after the one-year period had expired, Ortega was randomly contacting buyers via their mobile phones to learn about their experience to date. Handy Tider's buyer database, which included customer names and mobile phone numbers, was generated when buyers activated their product warranty online.

Ortega was in the process of contacting 500 purchasers who had owned the compactors for between one year and four years (when they had first been introduced) to determine whether the compactors had required repairs and, if so, the extent and cost of the repairs. In talking to purchasers, Ortega was impressed by the fact that there were remarkably few complaints involving the durability of the compactors.

Another type of complaint did arise, however, one that Ortega had difficulty understanding until he heard many buyers, usually from the same few cities, tell an almost identical story. It appears that in these cities the factory distributor would contact individuals who had purchased a standard model compactor from licensed retailers. The factory distributor would tell these buyers that the model originally requested was out of stock but that they could purchase a deluxe model for only $100 more than they originally paid for the standard model. The factory distributors also indicated that buyers would receive better after-sale service because higher-priced purchases would receive priority over lower-priced purchases if something malfunctioned. In addition, the factory distributors in these few cities indicated that they, not Handy Tider, Inc. stood behind the one-year warranty.

Ortega realized that he was uncovering a much larger — and more serious — problem than he had been assigned to explore. He chatted briefly with his supervisor, Sheryl Roger, who told Ortega to revise the format of his interview to include several questions concerning the installation. Roger also told Ortega to begin calling individuals who had owned compactors for less than a year. Ortega did this, and he discovered marked differences in the installation process based upon whether the customer purchased from a factory distributor or from a licensed retailer.

As a general rule, compactors purchased from factory distributors exhibited fast delivery in terms of elapsed time since sale. Importantly, over 90 percent of the deliveries occurred within the two-hour delivery windows that buyers were promised. Moreover, the installation personnel carefully explained how the compactor worked, and follow-up contacts were made to the customer three days and 10 days after installation to make certain that the customer had no additional questions concerning the compactor's operation.

On the other hand, Ortega learned of troubling inconsistencies in the delivery times of compactors purchased from licensed retailers. More specifically, fewer than 20 percent of the deliveries occurred within the two-hour delivery windows that buyers were promised. Even more disturbing was that in some cases the compactor was left in the middle of the kitchen floor in its shipping container — that is, uninstalled! Customers of the licensed retailers also indicated that installation personnel would not explain how the compactor worked and that some installers were rude and disrespectful. As an example, in response to one customer's question an installer stated, "Assuming you can read, the answer can be found in the owner's manual."

Ortega had another meeting scheduled with his supervisor. As Ortega entered Roger's office, he was surprised to see Handy Tider's vice president of marketing, Tom Bixby, also sitting in the office. Roger asked Ortega to tell Bixby the results of his interviews. After listening to Ortega, Bixby asked, "Do you think this pattern exists in all markets?"

"No," was Ortega's reply. "I'd say it is a problem in Jacksonville, Baltimore, Cleveland, Louisville, Denver, and San Diego. It may be a problem in Dallas and New Orleans. My sample wasn't very well structured in a metropolitan market sense; you will recall that it was a nationwide sample that was trying to look at repairs."

Questions for discussion

1. What should Handy Tider's vice president of marketing do? Why?
2. Discuss the pros and cons to allowing Handy Tider trash compactors to be sold only through licensed retailers.
3. Is it too late for Handy Tider to attempt service recovery with customers who reported a less-than-satisfactory installation experience? Why or why not?

New specialized terms

1. trash compactor   垃圾压缩机
2. landfill cost   垃圾填埋场本
3. factory distributor   工厂批发商
4. licensed retailer   特许零售商
5. warranty   保修期

Case summary

　　Handy Tider 公司是密苏里州圣路易斯市的一家垃圾压缩机制造商，产品行销全美国，其销售额的 90%集中于垃圾回收成本高的大城市。垃圾压缩机分为标准型与豪华型两种，两者尺寸相同，但后者的容量与功率更大。由于大多数放在厨房，公司生产了多款不同色彩与饰边的压缩机以便与厨房装饰灵活搭配。标准型与豪华型垃圾压缩机分别有 15 种、32 种的组合搭配，前者售价在$600 与$725 之间，后者售价在$950 与$1 100 之间。

　　Handy Tider 在每个大城市授权一家批发商负责向其特许零售商交付订单，同时也能直接销给最终顾客。每家批发商持有 Handy Tider 所有款式的垃圾压缩机存货，47 种款式的每一种至少储存 5 个单位。特许零售商因其零星销售特性及商品的花色品种多样而只维持每个款式的一或两件存货，他们的"设计你的梦想压缩机"软件能让顾客自行设计心仪的款式与色彩。零售商会把签下的订单发给 Handy Tider 最近的批发商。

　　按照批发商与 Handy Tider 签订的总协议，批发商接到特许零售商订单后的五天内必须送货与安装，其费用是单位批发价格的 9%，其中一半由特许零售商负担，一半由 Handy Tider 负担。

　　Handy Tider 配送部员工 Bob Ortega 正在研究是否将压缩机的保修期从一年延长到两年。垃圾压缩机的制造工艺良好，售出一年后几乎没有维修记录。Ortega 于是通过手机随机访问顾客，了解他们的最新使用体验。一旦买主在线激活产品保修证，他们的姓名与手机号将被录入买主数据库。Ortega 正在访问 500 位有一至四年压缩机使用经验的买主，以明确他们是否维修过压缩机，如果有，维修的程度与成本是多少。Ortega 印象最深的是，极少客户抱怨压缩机的耐用性。

　　然而，另一类很难直接了解到的抱怨与日俱增。Ortega 从少数几个城市的许多买主听到了几乎一样的故事。在这些城市，工厂批发商联系到那些从特许零售商处已经下了购买标准型压缩机订单的个人，言称该类产品缺货，如果加价 100 美元，可以买到豪华型压缩机。批发商还宣称，如果出了故障，高价购买的压缩机将比低价购买的享有更好的售后服务。而且，在这些少数城市，真正支持一年保修的是他们而不是 Handy Tider 公司。

　　Ortega 意识到他发现了比预想更大、更严重的问题，于是向其主管 Sheryl Roger 汇报了情况，后者让他修改访谈方案，加入一些涉及安装的问题。Roger 再令 Ortega 访问那些使用压缩机不到一年的客户。Ortega 进一步发现，客户从工厂批发商购买的压缩机与从特许零售商购买的压缩机，其安装过程差别甚大。

　　从工厂批发商购买的压缩机交货迅速，安装工还向顾客仔细解释工作原理，三天之后有回访；十天之后还会询问顾客操作是否存在问题。而从特许零售商购买的压缩机不仅交货慢，而且有时被置于厨房中央，既不给安装，也不解释工作原理，甚至粗暴无礼。面对顾客的质疑，一位安装工干脆回应说："你应该会看说明书，那里就能找到解决办法。"

　　Ortega 在另一次例行的与主管的见面会上，惊奇地看到 Handy Tider 的营销副总 Tom Bixby 也在场。Bixby 从 Ortega 的口中了解情况后，问道："所有市场上都存在这种现象吗？"

"不会"，Ortega 答道，"我认为问题发生在杰克逊维尔、巴尔的摩、克利夫兰、路易斯维尔、丹佛和圣迭戈，在达拉斯与新奥尔良也可能有。从大城市的市场层面判断，我的调查样本结构不够合理。您会想到，旨在考察维修事件的调研样本是个全国性的样本。"

Hint for analysis and Reference answer

1. What should Handy Tider's vice president of marketing do? Why?

The vice president of marketing should firstly conduct a thorough investigation on the problems caused by factory distributors. Secondly, he should empower Ortega to investigate the delivery and service failures in the case of licensed retailers. Thirdly, extend the sample to cover more large cities including New York, Los Angeles, Chicago, Houston, Phoenix, Philadelphia. Moreover, work with logistics managers to design a system to integrate the distribution network throughout the United States. If the vice president of marketing failed to take the above actions, things would get worse and the market share would decline quickly.

2. Discuss the pros and cons to allowing Handy Tider trash compactors to be sold only through licensed retailers.

The pros of allowing Handy Tider trash compactors to be sold only through licensed retailers are as follows:

(1) it is beneficial for Handy Tider to set up a location in its target city through licensed retailers.

(2) licensed retailers usually charge lower margins than distributors.

(3) Handy Tider can get efficient feedback from a retailer who knows its customers better.

The cons of allowing Handy Tider trash compactors to be sold only through licensed retailers:

(1) licensed retailers tend to sell a variety of goods supplied by other manufacturers and are less incentivized to sell Handy Tider's products because they normally hold less on-site stock;

(2) the service provided by these licensed retailers are relatively limited compared with factory distributors. They seldom provide extra services like marketing, branding, and labeling;

(3) the orders from licensed retailers are small which is not conducive to consolidating the transportation and distribution of trash compactors;

(4) it's difficult to build a close relationship between Handy Tider and its licensed retailers.

3. Is it too late for Handy Tider to attempt service recovery with customers who reported a less-than-satisfactory installation experience? Why or why not?

No, it is never too late for Handy Tider to attempt service recovery with customers.

Because Handy Tider has already dissatisfied its customers, who can leave Handy Tider forever or spread negative words of mouth of it if no actions are taken.

Effective service recovery is a key determinant of satisfaction, trust and commitment. Specific service recovery experience overwhelmed customer's cumulative prior experience in forming customer trust and commitment. Effective service recovery system can help Handy Tider gain competitive advantages by enhancing customer satisfaction and by spreading positive word of mouth. Besides, a sound service recovery system can also help to improve its employees' satisfaction and loyalty.

Case 6

DHL Logistics's Services Marketing Mix Efforts

In services industry, **marketing mix efforts**[1] hold an important place for positioning. As for logistics services industry, there exists thousands of logistics companies offering similar services. However, most of the companies prefer to work with a small number of logistics service providers that have good brand reputation or image. Hence, the logistics companies have begun to realize the impact of marketing efforts.

As a global leading mail and logistics company, DHL Group is focused on being the first choice for customers, employees and investors in its core business activities worldwide. It makes a positive contribution to the world by connecting people and enabling global trade while being committed to responsible business practices, purposeful environmental activities and corporate citizenship.

DHL' Product (Service) Strategy

For Logistics sector, in which DHL performs, it is crucial to provide different alternatives according to the variety of products which are to be transported. DHL Logistics aims offering variety of service options to its customers with 5 divisions, namely DHL Express, DHL Global Forwarding, DHL Freight, DHL Supply Chain and DHL Global Mail. DHL Express, one of the largest air carriers of the world, offers urgent documents and goods transportation to its customers while DHL Global Forwarding division offers air, ocean, rail and road freight options to its customers in addition to warehousing and distribution opportunities. Freight division of the company supplies road and rail freight with LTL (**less than truck load**[2]), FTL (**full truck load**[3]) and intermodal services options and DHL Supply Chain provides warehousing, managed-transport and value-added services. Ultimately, DHL Global Mail division offers customized mail and B2C parcel shipments. Customers may take advantage of standardized, traditional or specially-designed freight options. Since DHL aims to build long-term partnerships and provide wide range of transportation options, the company provides diverse industry sector solutions targeting different fields such as aerospace, automotive, chemical, consumer, fashion, healthcare, retail, technology, manufacturing and renewable energy. There also exist standardized service options; nevertheless, they can be customized according to specific demands of the clients.

The characteristics of the goods shipped, delivery lead times and criticality of the freight to ultimate consumers are the main factors in service type determination. For instance, the logistics processes of cars are different from chemicals and medications, not only in terms of lead times but also the way of carriage and warehousing (i.e. temperature-controlled freight, cold storage).

DHL' Price Strategy

For standardized freight services, DHL Logistics prefers implementing **cost plus pricing strategy**[4] which covers deciding on final price by adding a percentage to costs as a profit margin. In accordance with the state of the market, if needed, DHL Logistics implements competition pricing strategy and sets the final price in comparison with its competitors. Additionally, since channel members set different prices for different destinations, the price of the provided transportation service differs in accordance with the distance of the destination.

For customized services, prices are relatively high when compared with standardized transportation services provided by the company. In other words, company implements **premium pricing strategy**[5] for specially-designed service options. Nonetheless, via special contracts, DHL offers special prices to its loyal customers and the most important companies of the market.

DHL' Promotion Strategy

DHL usually prefers introducing its service offerings through television advertisements. Additionally, DHL holds several sponsorship deals with some of the most exclusive worldwide events such as Rugby World Cup, Formula 1, IMG Fashion Week, Manchester United, Barclays Premiere League and Gewandhaus Orchestra. These sponsorships are carefully selected by DHL with the intention of reflecting the values of the company. For instance, the reason behind being sponsor of IMG Fashion Week is given as the relationship between DHL's motto "Tailor made" and fashion industry.

Advertising through mass media and traditional manners is complemented by public relations, with the purpose of generating a positive image of a company in the market and society preferably through editorial text. In this order, DHL also shows its presence with social responsibility projects such as "Go Green". With slogan "Good For The Environment & Good For Business", company strives to provide carbon efficiency performance guideline and diminish the possible environmental harms created by logistics industry.

DHL' Place Strategy

DHL has numerous branches all around the world in addition to its own DHL Network of Express Logistics Centers (8 DHL-operated and -managed facilities located worldwide). DHL's "globally centralized points of distribution" increases the company's efficiency. DHL has 850 terminals, warehouses and offices located in approximately 150 territories. Express conducts its operations in more than 220 countries and territories with a fleet of more than 250 aircraft.

DHL Global Forwarding division provides distribution opportunity in more than 150 countries and territories and freight division of the company offers service options in excess of 50 countries and territories and in excess of 180 terminals. Supply Chain division offers services options approximately in 60 countries and territories and has 2,590 warehouses, terminals and offices all around the world. Finally, DHL Global Mail has 32 sales offices, 26 processing centers on 5 continents with direct connections in more than 200 countries. Regarding the selection criteria of distribution channel members, DHL selects channel members based on several criteria such as service quality, costs and facilities. Some customer freights may require special equipment and carriage. For instance, when perishable goods such as chemicals or food are transported, shipping firms which offer cold options are selected, or to ship hazardous materials, those airlines that have authorization of hazardous material transportation are chosen. It can be said that the most significant expectation of DHL from its channel members is meeting promised requirements.

DHL' Physical Evidence[6]

Since corporate identity is reinforced by logos and symbols, DHL uses its widely-known logo, red DHL writing on a yellow-colored-base, and yellow color on its trucks, packaging materials and buildings. Moreover, company attaches great importance to the design of its website, brochures, business cards and even invoices. They all have carefully selected designs and reflect DHL's brand identity with yellow logo and the name of the company written in red.

For employees working at internal operation departments, there exists no dress code due to the reason that they are not directly communicating with customers. Since company believes that lack of a strict dress code for these employees increase their performance, employees working at internal operations departments are able to dress in business casual style. However, employees who are working at sales, operations, and human resources departments and employees who are involved in customer visits are obliged to obey written dress code.

DHL' People

At DHL, personnel training is a very crucial aspect. Before starting to work for DHL, every employee of DHL has to attend to the New Employee Orientation Program that aims introducing all products of DHL to employees and developing their communication skills. In addition to new employee orientation, all of the beginner employees are obliged to receive training of Code of Conduct, Policy of Information Assurance, Adaptation to Competition and Fight Against Corruption within first three months. Separately, all employees receive trainings, which are related with their departments, i.e. MS Office, communication techniques, multidimensional leadership etc. Moreover, since the company uses a SAP based IT program, all of the employees get training regarding the usage of Interalia system. Additional department-based trainings are being arranged in accordance with needs of departments such as sales, product, customer relations and operation.

DHL' Processes

DHL pays attention to the integration of computer programs for measuring customer satisfaction and being able to inform customers about processes. Through the medium of Soft Trans program, the company measures duration of cargo handling. Problems regarding cargo handling are being measured via questionnaires in certain time periods. Complaints and customer opinions are being recorded routinely. Received complaints are being categorized according to related subtitles and the company endeavors to develop solutions to satisfy customers' demands as fast as possible in order to prevent customer losses. In a similar vein, I-sell program is being used for keeping records of customer visits and sales reports.

DHL Logistics provides diversified customer service strategies based on the type of customer. For instance, DHL offers 7/24/365 customer service for specific industries such as aerospace industry in which the delivery is being done within business hours. Based on the emergency, different delivery options can be preferred by different industries.

For recovering any encountered operational problem, DHL undertakes additional costs in order to relief and maintain customer loyalty. Every occurred problem is being recorded into the system and customers are being informed about the solution process. Through this system, they can track the status of the freight or the stage of solution process. Even it's a customer's fault, DHL tries to solve the problem as soon as possible with the lowest additional cost reflected to the customer. If a problem occurs after DHL delivers its clients' freight to the air freight service provider, company opens a claim and for any occurred damage or loss, legal process that is stated in the back of the **bill of lading**[7] is followed with the carrier.

Questions for discussion

1. Why is it necessary for logistics companies to emphasize services marketing mix?
2. Why physical evidence is so important to logistics companies?
3. What does "people" strategy focus on?

New specialized terms

1. marketing mix effort　营销组合措施
2. less than truck load　拼车货
3. full truck load　整车货
4. cost plus pricing strategy　成本加成定价策略
5. premium pricing strategy　高溢价策略
6. physical evidence　有形展示
7. bill of lading　提单

Case summary

DHL 物流的服务营销组合措施

在服务行业，营销组合对市场定位至关重要。具体到物流服务业，会有成千上万的物流公司提供类似的服务，但是大多数公司更愿意与少数具有良好品牌声誉或形象的物流服务提供商合作。鉴于此，物流公司已经意识到营销组合的重要影响。

作为全球领先的邮递与物流公司，DHL 集团致力于成为客户、员工与核心业务遍及全球的投资者的首选。DHL 争当责任感强、注重环保的企业公民，通过连接大众、促进全球贸易为世界作出积极贡献。

DHL 的产品（服务）策略

在 DHL 所从事的物流行业，根据要运输的产品种类提供不同的运输方式至关重要。DHL 物流的目标是为客户提供各种服务选择，包括 DHL 快运、DHL 全球货运、DHL 运输、DHL 供应链和 DHL 全球邮递等 5 个部门。DHL 快运是世界上最大的航空公司之一，为客户提供紧急文件和货物运输服务，而 DHL 全球货运部门除了提供仓储和配送服务外，还为客户提供空运、海运、铁路和公路货运选择。该公司的货运部门提供公路、铁路货运的 LTL（拼车货）、FTL（整车货）运输以及多式联运服务，DHL 供应链提供仓储、运输管控和增值服务。DHL 全球邮递部门提供定制邮件和 B2C 包裹运输。客户可以选用标准化的或特别设计的货运。由于 DHL 旨在建立长期合作伙伴关系并提供广泛的运输选择，该公司提供针对不同领域的各种解决方案，如航空航天、汽车、化工、消费、时尚、医疗保健、零售、科技、制造和可再生能源，还有标准化的服务选择。尽管如此，它们还可以根据客户的具体要求进行定制。

物品特性，前置期长短与运输队最终客户的重要性都是影响服务类型决策的主要因素。例如，汽车物流的流程在前置期、运输方式、仓储要求（温控运输、冷藏）等方面不同于化工与医疗物资。

DHL 的价格策略

对于标准化货运服务，DHL 物流更倾向于采用成本加成定价策略，即在成本基础上加上一定百分比的利润率作为最终价格。根据市场状况，如果需要，DHL 物流实施竞争导向定价策略，即参照竞争对手确定最终价格。另外，不同的目的地设置不同的价格，所提供的运输服务的价格根据目的地的距离而不同。对于定制服务，与公司提供的标准化运输服务相比，价格相对较高。换句话说，公司为特别设计的服务选项实施高价策略。尽管如此，依据特殊合同，DHL 为其忠实的客户和市场上最重要的公司提供特价。

DHL 的促销策略

DHL 通常喜欢通过电视广告介绍其服务产品。此外，DHL 还举办了多项赞助活动，举办了一些全球最独特的活动，如橄榄球世界杯、一级方程式、IMG 时装周、曼联、巴克莱英超联赛和 Gewandhaus 交响乐会。这些赞助由 DHL 精心挑选，旨在反映公司的价值观。例如，之所以赞助 IMG 时装周是因为 DHL 的座右铭"精准定制"和时尚产业密切相关。通过公关活动配合大众媒体和传统广告，目的是通过社论式的文案在市场和社会上树立公司的正面形象。DHL 还通过参与"Go Green"等社会责任项目树立形象。公司的口号是"利于商业，利于环境"，致力于以低碳原则提升绩效，减少物流行业可能造成的环境危害。

DHL 的分销策略

除了自己的 DHL 快递物流中心网络（全球 8 个 DHL 运营和管理的设施）外，DHL 在全球拥有众多分支机构，其"全球集中分销点"提高了公司的效率。DHL 在大约 150 个地区拥有 850 个场站、仓库和办事处。快运公司在超过 220 个国家和地区开展业务，拥有 250 多架飞机。DHL 全球货运部门在 150 多个国家和地区提供分销机会，公司的货运部门提供超过 50 个国家和地区以及超过 180 个场站的服务选择。供应链部门在大约 60 个国家和地区提供服务选择，在全球拥有 2 590 个仓库、场站和办事处。最后，DHL 全球邮递在五大洲设有 32 个销售办事处和 26 个加工中心，在 200 多个国家拥有直营网点。DHL 根据服务质量、成本和设施等几个标准选择渠道成员。一些客户货物可能需要特殊设备和运输，例如，易腐产品要选择冷链运输企业，危险品要选择那些有危险品运输资质的航空公司。可以说，DHL 对其渠道成员的最重要期望是满足承诺的要求。

DHL 的"有形展示"策略

鉴于徽标和符号可以加强企业形象，DHL 使用其广为人知的徽标——在黄色背景上的红色 DHL 图案。其卡车、包装材料和建筑物上都采用黄色。此外，公司非常重视网站、宣传册、名片甚至发票的设计，用黄色商标和红色公司名称反映 DHL 的品牌标识。内勤员工由于不需要直接与客户沟通，可以穿商务休闲装。但是，在销售部门、运营部门和人力资源部门工作的员工以及参与客户拜访的员工都有义务按公司文化搭配着装。

DHL 的人本管理

在 DHL，人员培训是一个非常关键的方面。在开始为 DHL 工作之前，DHL 的每位员工都必须参加新员工入职培训计划，该计划旨在向员工介绍 DHL 的所有产品并培养他们的沟通技巧。除了入职培训外，所有初级员工都有义务在头三个月内接受"行为准则""信息保障政策""适应竞争和反腐败"等培训。另外，所有员工都接受与其部门相关的培训，即 MS Office、通信技术、多维领导等。此外，由于公司使用基于 SAP 的 IT 计划，所有员工都接受有关 Interalia 系统使用的培训。

DHL 的流程管理

DHL 注重整合计算机程序，以测量客户满意度并能够把流程通知客户。公司通过 Soft Trans 计划测算货物处理的持续时间，而通过问卷调查检测有关货物处理的问题。公司还会记录投诉和客户意见，收到的投诉根据相关标题进行分类，并努力开发解决方案，以尽快满足客户的需求，防止客户流失。类似地，I-sell 计划用于保存客户访问和销售报告的记录。DHL 物流根据客户类型提供多元化的客户服务策略。例如，DHL 为特定行业提供

7/24/365 客户服务，例如航空航天业，其交货在工作时间内完成。根据紧急情况，不同行业可以选择不同的交付方式。在遇到运营问题的情况下，DHL 承担额外费用以弥补和维持客户忠诚度。每个发生的问题都会被记录到系统中，并且告知客户解决方案和过程。通过该系统，他们可以跟踪货运状态或问题解决过程所处的阶段。即使是客户的错误，DHL 也会尽快解决问题，只向客户收取最低的额外成本。如果 DHL 将客户的货物运抵空运服务商之后出现了问题，公司会根据提单背后的条款依法要求承运商赔偿客户发生的损失。

Hint for analysis and Reference answer

1. Why is it necessary for logistics companies to emphasize services marketing mix?

The services marketing mix has an incontrovertible importance for creating a mental picture of intangible products, in other words services. In a similar vein, when logistics sector's disadvantageous position in Porter's Five Forces of Competition Model is considered, it ought to emphasize the importance of positioning decisions and marketing mix efforts for logistics service providers.

2. Why physical evidence is so important to logistics companies?

Components of physical layout such as odors, colors, temperature, noise level, and comfort of furnishings may influence the perceived performance of service provider. Organizations operating in services industry should emphasize on physical evidence when establishing service standards, because the tangible evidence and the attitude of the customer specifies the ultimate quality of the service experience. Besides, before buying the service, customers judge a service by the tangible clues that surround it.

3. What does "people" strategy focus on?

People-oriented strategy attaches great importance on employee satisfaction. (Hint: think about the theory of service profit chain)

Part Three

Transportation Management

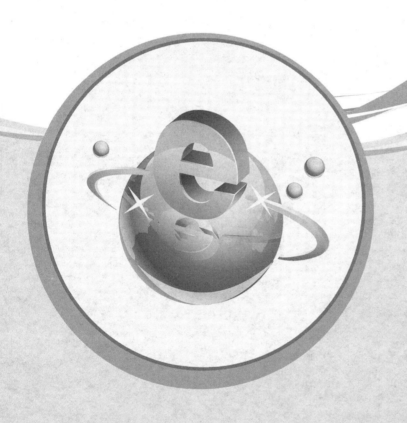

Part Three Transportation Management

After learning this part, you will be able to:
- Gain an understanding of the characteristics of various modes of transportation
- Explain transportation strategy in an integrated logistics context
- Get an overview of transportation principles and their implication for carriers and shippers
- Explain operations in a variety of transportation settings.

Case 7

Coals to Newcastle

The Blizzard Steamship Company, headquartered in Hampton Roads, Virginia, had been asked to bid on a **contract of affreightment**[1] for the carriage of several million tons of coal from Hampton Roads to an English port, where the coal would be unloaded and then move by rail to Newcastle. (Contracts of affreightment are used when a shipper has vast quantities of materials to move, often over a period of several years and requiring several vessels provided on a charter basis. The owners of the charter vessels, such as Blizzard, assign various vessels in their fleet to participate in the haulage.)

One of the vessels in Blizzard's fleet, the Jennifer Young, was ideally suited for this assignment, and Blizzard decided to determine first how much coal she could carry over a 12-month period, at which point he could decide which other vessel(s) to assign. There were no **backhauls**[2] available so the vessel would sail light from England back to Hampton Roads.

The anticipated costs of operating the Jennifer Young follow. Days in port cost $1,000 each and days at sea cost $2,000 each. At sea there is also the **cost of bunkers**[3] (fuel oil), which is expected to be $50 per ton. Fuel consumption per nautical mile of travel increases exponentially with the vessel's speed. All assumptions include a day in port at Hampton Roads for loading and two days at the English port for unloading. While the vessel is returning to the United States light, it is traveling against prevailing weather, so it takes the same number of days to cross in each direction. (Table 3-1)

The vessel, when loaded, is loaded as heavily as allowed by the insurer. If it carries less fuel it can carry more cargo. Hence, calculations for travel at slower speeds will show a slightly higher tonnage of coal carried per voyage. Table 3-1 shows the duration of a round trip (including three days in ports) and the load of coal and fuel carried.

Table 3-1 Duration of round trip and the load of coal and fuel carried

Duration of round trip in days	Fuel carried (and consumed) in tons	Tons of coal carried
14	600	60,000
15	500	60,100
16	420	60,180
17	350	60,250
18	300	60,300
19	240	60,360
20	200	60,400

▶ Questions for discussion

1. How many round trips should the vessel make if the objective is to haul the most coal within one year? (The number of voyages can include a fraction, since this would mean that a portion of the last voyage would be completed in the first days of the following year.)
2. How many round trips should the vessel make if the objective is to haul the coal at the lowest cost per ton within one year? (The number of voyages can include a fraction, since this would mean that a portion of the last voyage would be completed in the first days of the following year.)
3. Does it make a difference where the vessel is located before it is assigned to begin work on this haul?
4. Assume that the price of oil drops to $25 per ton. How, if at all, does this change your answer to one?
5. Assume that the price of oil drops to $10 per ton. How, if at all, does this change your answer to two?

▶ New specialized terms

1. contract of affreightment   货运合同
2. backhaul   回程货
3. cost of bunkers   燃油成本

Case summary

运往纽卡斯尔的煤

总部位于弗吉尼亚州汉普顿路的 Blizzard 船公司被邀参加一个几百万吨煤的运输合同项目竞标。这批煤要先从汉普顿路运到一个英国港口，在港口换装，再通过铁路运到纽卡斯尔。

Blizzard 的船队之一 Jennifer Young 公司很适合此次运输任务。Blizzard 需要先确定在 12 月的周期内能运送多少煤，再决定在哪个结点派哪些船只前往。由于没有回程货，从英格兰到汉普顿路的商船是空驶的。Jennifer Young 公司预计的运营成本如下：船舶在港一天费用 1 000 美元，在海上航行一天费用 2 000 美元，燃油费用每吨 50 美元。船行速度提高，燃油消耗会加倍增加。所有假设中都包括汉普顿港的 1 天装船时间与英国港口的 2 天卸船时间。返回美国的船只虽然是空载，但由于是逆风航行，行驶时间与去程相同（见表 3–1）。

按投保约定，船只可以满载。每次航运装载的燃油减少，装载的货物便会增加。因此，船速减慢，每次可装载的煤量会增加。表 3-1 列出了一次往返的时间（包括在港口的 3 天）、装载的燃料数量与运煤量。

▶ **Hint for analysis and Reference answer**

1. How many round trips should the vessel make if the objective is to haul the most coal within one year?

(1) 365/14=26.1(次);　26×60,000=1,560,000(ton)

(2) 365/15=24.3(次)　24×60,100=1,442,400(ton)

……

(7) 365/20=18.3(次)　18×60,400=1,087,200(ton)

Therefore, the vessel should make 26.1 round trips if the objective is to haul the most coal within one year (1,560,000 tons is the biggest).

2. How many round trips should the vessel make if the objective is to haul the coal at the lowest cost per ton within one year?

(1) duration of round trip is 14 days:

total cost=26.1(600×50+3×1,000+11×2,000)=1,435,500($)

(2) duration of round trip is 15 days:

total cost=24.3(500×50+3×1,000+12×2,000)=1,263,600($)

……

(7) duration of round trip is 20 days:

total cost=18.3(200×50+3×1,000+17×2,000)= 857,750($)

Therefore, the vessel should make 18.3 round trips if the objective is to haul the coal at the lowest cost per ton within one year ($ 0.776 is the lowest cost.)

3. Does it make a difference where the vessel is located before it is assigned to begin work on this haul?

Yes, it will make a difference where the vessel is located before it is assigned to begin work on this haul. Assume the vessel is located at American port, the total cost of transporting coals will differ a lot.

4. Assume that the price of oil drops to $25 per ton. How, if at all, does this change your answer to one?

No change. The answer is the same to question one.

5. Assume that the price of oil drops to $10 per ton. How, if at all, does this change your answer to two?

We will change the answer to question two. The round trip the vessel should make is 14 days (26 times) because the cost per ton is the lowest ($ 0.517).

Part Three   Transportation Management

Case 8

H. Stevens Inc.

H. Stevens Inc. has operated in the United States for sixty years. The firm's primary business was marketing and selling **fast-moving consumer goods**[1] and medicines, but upper management saw additional opportunities in third-party logistics. In 2015, the firm's two sales divisions each operated its own logistics team, and Stevens also run a fleet of twenty-five vehicles. Management saw an increasing demand for integrated logistics services. Many of its customers had inefficient and costly logistics operations and were looking for ways to reduce costs and improve service. Several customers lacked experience in operating large-scale warehousing and distribution functions.

In February 2015, Stevens established a new logistics division to design integrated logistics systems for other firms. Management decided to treat the new division as a profit center.

In May 2015, Leewick Ltd, a multinational food and household products company, contracted with Stevens for logistics services. Six months later another multinational medicine and nutritional manufacturer, Nutricare Ltd, entered into a similar contract with Stevens.

According to the agreements, logistics assets and personnel could be transferred to Stevens when they took over the operation. A few warehousing employees from both multinational firms joined Stevens but most continued to work for their respective companies. To ensure a smooth transition to third-party operations, transportation teams from Leewick and Nutricare were managed and supervised independently according to their old practices.

Stevens had four fleets: A, B, C, D. Fleet A took care of the fast-moving consumer goods and **bulk delivery**[2]. Fleet A served supermarkets and small stores, selling household and food products. Fleet B delivered medicines to doctors and hospitals. Fleet C was the **ex-Leewick delivery team**[3], serving customers similar to the customers of Fleet A. Fleet D was the ex-Nutricare delivery team, serving **dispensary stores**[4], hospitals, and supermarkets. (See Table 3-2 and 3-3 for fleet information.)

Table 3-2　Transportation Fleet Structure

Type of service/Vehicle Size	Type	Fleet A	Fleet B	Fleet C	Fleet D	Total	Estimated Capacity per week/t
Expedite	Van	0	5	0	0	5	20
Small	Box	9	4	4	4	21	60
12 meter	Box	3	0	1	0	4	80
15 meter	Box	4	0	2	0	6	120
	Total	16	9	7	4	36	280

Table 3-3　Transportation Department Organization

Fleet A	Fleet B	Fleet C	Fleet D
1 supervisor	1 supervisor	1 supervisor	1 supervisor
2 ass't supervisors[5]	1 ass't supervisor	1 ass't supervisor	1 clerk
3 clerks	2 clerks	1 clerk	4 drivers
16 drivers	9 drivers	7 drivers	8 helpers
32 helpers	18 helpers	14 helpers	
54 employees	31 employees	24 employees	14 employees

After almost twelve months of operation, Stevens' clients are satisfied with the logistics services, but profits are lower than expected. The final account for 2016 shows that the overall profit of the **integrated logistics division**[6] was well below budget. The shortfall was attributed to losses incurred by the transportation department. The general manager of the division has asked the transportation manager to take immediate action to improve the efficiency of the transportation department and to achieve cost savings.

Questions for discussion

1. What steps should be taken to bring the transport services back to profitability? Why?
2. Special care is one of the major customer service elements and strategies. How can you strike a balance between delivery costs and customer service levels?

New specialized terms

1. fast-moving consumer goods　快消品
2. bulk delivery　大批量地送货
3. ex-Leewick delivery team　原有的 Leewick 送货车队
4. dispensary store　药房
5. ass't supervisor　主管助理
6. integrated logistics division　整合物流部

Case summary

史蒂文斯公司

史蒂文斯公司在美国经营了60多年。该公司的主要业务是营销、销售快消品和药品，但高层管理人员在第三方物流方面看到了更多机会。2015年，该公司的两个销售部门各自运营着自己的物流团队，而史蒂文斯也拥有25辆车。管理层对整合物流服务的需求不断增加。许多客户的物流运营效率低下且成本高昂，他们正在寻找降低成本和改善服务的方法。一些客户缺乏运营大型仓储和配送业务的经验。

2015年2月，史蒂文斯成立了一个新的物流部门，旨在为其他公司设计整合物流系统。管理层决定将新部门视为利润中心。2015年5月，一家跨国食品和家居用品公司Leewick公司与史蒂文斯签订了物流服务合同。6个月后，另一家跨国医药和营养品制造商Nutricare公司与史蒂文斯签订了类似的合同。

根据协议，物流资产和人员在业务接管时可以转让给史蒂文斯。来自两家跨国公司的一些仓储员工加入了史蒂文斯，但大多数继续为各自的公司工作。为了确保顺利过渡到第三方运营，史蒂文斯仍然根据他们的老做法独立管理和监督Leewick和Nutricare的运输团队。史蒂文斯拥有四支车队：A、B、C、D。车队A负责快消品和散货并服务于超市和销售家居用品和食品的小商店；车队B向医生和医院提供药品；车队C是前Leewick的送货团队，服务的客户类似A车队；车队D是前Nutricare的送货团队，为药房、医院和超市提供服务。

经过近12个月的运营，史蒂文斯的客户对物流服务感到满意，但其利润低于预期。2016年的最终账户显示整合物流部的整体利润远低于预算，此差距归因于运输部门的损失。该部门的总经理要求运输经理立即采取行动，以提高运输部门的效率，并实现成本节约。

Hint for analysis and Reference answer

1. What steps should be taken to bring the transport services back to profitability? Why?

Firstly, H. Stevens should strengthen the integration of logistics division by making warehouse employees from both multinational firms conform to its new rules, manage the newly-built transportation teams in a coherent way. Secondly, restructure the transportation department according to the nature of goods transported or the target customers, for example, merge Fleet C with Fleet A, Fleet D with Fleet B or establish a new fleet providing special service for fresh foods to supermarkets. Thirdly, pay attention to operating controls and conduct marketing research to find new customers and search back haul shipments for the sake of reducing overall distribution cost.

2. Special care is one of the major customer service elements and strategies. How can you strike a balance between delivery costs and customer service levels?

The top management of H. Stevens might consider taking the following measures to strike a balance between delivery costs and customer service levels:

(1) implementing a differentiation strategy — provide different services to different customers;

(2) leveraging management skills and advanced technologies such as TMS, EDI, CRM, CPFR, JIT delivery, etc.

(3) strengthening systematic operational information exchange with customers like supermarkets and hospitals.

(4) building strong corporate culture, such as, advocating democratic management style; empower front-line employees more rights to serve customers; make all employees work as a team to create values for customers, etc.

Case 9

Ocean spray-shipping products more efficiently

Ocean Spray, an **agricultural cooperative**[1] owned by more than 700 cranberry growers in North America and Chile, and 35 Florida grapefruit growers, is one of North America's largest producers of bottled juices and juice drinks. The company is constantly redesigning its transportation networks to better serve their customers and reduce transportation costs. Because demand for its products in the Southeast was growing, Ocean Spray decided to open a new distribution center in Lakeland, Florida, in 2011. By centralizing supply closer to clients, the company had already slashed millions of miles out of its **distribution network**[2], cutting both **freight costs**[3] and **carbon emissions**[4].

But soon after that, Ocean Spray was approached by Wheels Clipper, an Illinois-based third-party logistics service provider (3PL) that specializes in intermodal, truckload, and **refrigerated shipping**[5]. The 3PL had an intriguing business proposition for the cooperative. One of its clients, Tropicana, which is also one of Ocean Spray's competitors in the fruit juice business, was already shipping fresh fruit by boxcar on trains from Florida to New Jersey — and sending empty boxcars back to Florida. Since much of Ocean Spray's Lakeland-bound freight originated in Bordentown, N.J., Wheels Clipper suggested that Ocean Spray could take advantage of that backhaul capacity.

Ocean Spray decided Wheels Clipper's proposal was worth pursuing. After looking into the matter further, it determined it could indeed take advantage of the backhaul opportunity — though it would require a few minor adjustments in its shipping patterns. "One thing we had to look at was our **load planning**[6]," Young recalls. Each truckload shipment held 19 pallets of goods, but boxcars handle 38. "We had to take that into consideration in our **order fulfillment**[7] planning," she says, "We had to do a little bit of work on the pallet size and the configuration of the pallets."

Delivery schedules[8] also required some adjustments. Shipping goods by truck takes three days, while the journey by rail takes four to five days. That meant asking the Florida DC to carry more inventory than it might otherwise have done. The payoff, however, promised to be enormous. The arrangement that was eventually put in place resulted in Ocean Spray's shifting '80 percent of the New Jersey-to-Florida shipments to rail over a 12-month period, yielding reductions in both shipping costs and emissions. By using Tropicana's backhaul capacity, Ocean Spray's shifting 80 percent of the New Jersey-to-Florida shipments to rail over a 12-month period, and result in 40% reduction in transportation costs for this lane and 68% reduction in CO_2 emissions.

▶ Questions for discussion

1. How did the company reduce the transportation cost?
2. What are the impacts of the switch from road to rail on a company's distribution network? Are there fundamental elements for successful shift?

▶ New specialized words

1. agricultural cooperative　农业合作社
2. distribution network　配送网络
3. freight costs　运输成本
4. carbon emission　碳排放
5. refrigerated shipping　冷链运输
6. load planning　装载计划
7. order fulfillment　订单履行
8. delivery schedule　交货时间表

Case summary

优鲜沛——更高效的运输

优鲜沛是一家由北美和智利的700多位蔓越莓种植者及35家佛罗里达葡萄柚种植者拥有的农业合作社组织，是北美最大的瓶装果汁及果饮的生产商之一。该公司不断改进其运输网络以更好地服务客户，降低运输成本。随着美国东南部需求的增加，该公司决定于2011年在佛罗里达开设配送中心，通过更贴近顾客，该公司大大减少了运输里程，降低了运费和碳排放。

此后不久，一家位于伊利诺伊州专营公路、多式联运与冷藏运输的第三方物流企业发现，优鲜沛在果汁领域的竞争对手之一——纯果乐在用火车把果汁从佛罗里达运到新泽西，然后空箱返回。由于该空返方向和优鲜沛的运输方向一致，该第三方物流企业建议优鲜沛利用这些回程运力。优鲜沛认为该提议有合理性，发现通过一些轻微调整就可以利用这种回程运力。优鲜沛的运输经理回忆："我们要考虑装载计划。"公路整车每车运19个托盘货，火车车厢能运38个。"我们需要考虑订单履行计划"，她说。"我们需要改变托盘批量和托盘的配置。"交货时间表也需要调整，公路运输需要 3 天，铁路运输需要 4 到 5 天，这意味着佛罗里达配送中心会持有更高的库存。变革的成效非常显著，12 个月的时间内优鲜沛 80%由新泽西运往佛罗里达的货物转为铁路运输，这条线路上运输成本降低了 40%，碳排放降低了 68%。

▷ Hint for analysis and Reference answer

1. How did the company reduce the transportation cost?

The underlying reason is that the company is always thinking about redesigning its transportation network. The setup of Florida DC helps shorten the transportation distance, thus transportation cost is lowered. Furthermore, by making use of the empty backhaul of rail transport of a competitor, the company has shifted from road to rail in one route, which leads to lower transportation cost.

2. What are the impacts of the switch from road to rail on a company's distribution network? Are there fundamental elements for successful shift?

At least two results are incurred: with longer transition time in rail transport, inventory level at both ends of the route will increase, which requires larger storage space; rail transport is terminal-to-terminal transport, which needs the connection of road transport.

Rail shipping works well for products that move in fairly regular volumes, so Ocean Spray's shipments should be constant and continuous. Second, Ocean Spray should have large DCs to keep more inventory. Third, Ocean spray's DCs should not be far away from rail terminals, otherwise the shift would be meaningless.

Part Four

Warehousing and Inventory Management

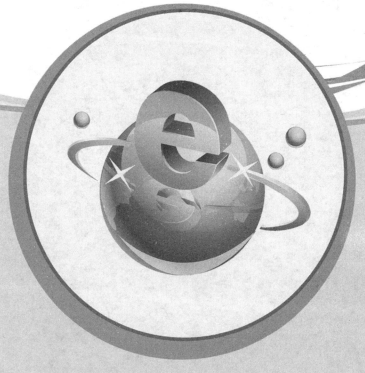

Part Four Warehousing and Inventory Management

Learning Objectives

After learning this part, you will be able to:
- Explain the main functions of warehousing and inventory management
- Gain an understanding of the objectives of and approaches to inventory management
- Get an overview of classification models used by firms
- Discuss activity-based costing in a logistics context

Case 10

Implementing CMI at the Whitbread Beer Company

The Whitbread Beer Company is the brewing division of Whitbread Plc, the brewing, leisure and drinks retailing group. The group is one of the UK's leading brewers, with an extensive portfolio of pubs, restaurant chains and hotels. It is also the largest owner of **high-street off-licenses**[1] in the country. Its brewing interests were formally separated from the group's extensive on-trade retailing interests in response to the Monopolies and Mergers Commission's 1992 "Beer Orders".

Nevertheless, the Beer Company continues to manage the supply of its own beers and a range of third-party produced drinks to the group's on-trade and off-trade retail networks, as well as to other third-party retailers — mainly the large **grocery multiples**[2].

The changing demands of the marketplace have meant that The Whitbread Beer Company, like most of its competitors, has diversified its product portfolio, but the proliferation of new brands has created complications for the manufacturing side of the brewing business, which is geared to large batch runs. Pressure to optimize production could lead to high stocks of finished product, which become difficult to manage when dispersed through an extensive distribution system. This in turn could threaten product quality, resulting in problems with shelf life, particularly for the low-volume premium bands.

Whitbread had been gradually reorganizing and rationalizing its drinks logistics structure since the early 1990s, to develop a more efficient and flexible network, wherever possible Whitbread's own product inventory was consolidated and moved back upstream within the network. Meanwhile, just-in-time deliveries were introduced from the group's own manufacturing sites to its 3,850 pubs and inns, and to its 1,524 high-street off-licenses. In 1995, falling beer prices in the off-trade led Whitbread to investigate the possibility of further reducing stock holdings within its own distribution network by moving major third-party suppliers of drinks for resale onto **Co-Managed Inventory (CMI)**[3] agreements. It was believed that the introduction of CMI could ease the stress on Whitbread's own business, while improving stock availability and affecting a top-change in lead-time and order cycle reduction.

As a first step overture was made to Whitbread's largest volume off-trade supplier, US-based Anheuser. Anheuser is the Goliath of the international brewing industry, controlling a massive 45 percent of its domestic market. It is widely recognized as having the lowest inventories of any major US brewer and prides itself on the freshness of its products. Whitbread is Anheuser's largest customer in the United Kingdom, with four of its products accounting for 9 percent of Whitbread's off-trade sales, so there were critical mass benefits for both sides. Anheuser's expertise and the fact that its trade with Whitbread was relatively predictable, involving high volumes and low **SKUs**[4], made the US brewer an ideal pilot partner. The two companies adopted an EDI facilitated partnership approach for the project, with GE Information Services as its network supplier.

Under the pilot program Whitbread provided Anheuser with a 13-week rolling forecast, along with daily updates of Anheuser's distribution centers. These told Anheuser what Whitbread was planning to sell and let the supplier know what had actually been sold on a day-by-day basis. Anheuser was then allowed to determine what to ship in terms of mix and quantity, provided that stocks stayed within pre-determined stock bands (usually 2-4 days) and in line with an agreed overall product mix. This flexibility allowed the supplier to manage its production and transport planning to best effect. Whitbread required 24 hours' notice ahead of delivery as a safeguard, but was pleased to discover that on no occasion throughout the first year of CMI trading was it necessary to amend a supplier raised order.

The pilot reduced Whitbread's stock of Anheuser products from 8 to 4 days, while service levels rose from 98.6 percent to 99.3 percent. The fact that Whitbread produces a number of substitute products gave Anheuser a strong incentive not to allow **stock-outs**[5] to occur. Some inventory was displaced to the supplier, but inventory levels within the system as a whole were reduced. Anheuser benefited from access to better forecasting and sales information, and better utilization of assets. As a CMI supplier it received preferential treatment in the allocation of **prime-time overnight delivery slots**[6] and was allowed to deliver mixed consignments in full truck-loads. The regularity and volume of the shipments—three per day to each of Whitbread's five distribution center—meant that further transport efficiencies could be realized by **back-loading vehicles**[7]. The Anheuser pilot was fully live by March 1996.

Part Four Warehousing and Inventory Management

In July 1996, Whitbread held a supplier conference for the top seven of its 72 suppliers, to share the knowledge gained from the CMI pilot and discuss the extension of the program. These 10 percent of suppliers account for 50 percent of Whitbread's inventory costs, 60 percent of sales by volume, 55 percent of invoice volume and 80 percent of invoice value (there are just over 500 product lines between the entire supplier base). Whitbread estimated that rolling the CMI program out to include the other six top suppliers would achieve a one-off stock reduction of £1.4 million. Moreover, lower inventories meant smaller depots and fewer distribution centers, resulting in substantial savings in the longer term.

By late 1996, two of Whitbread's other leading suppliers, soft drinks manufacturer Britvic and rival brewers Guinness, were well on the way to joining Anheuser with full CMI between themselves and Whitbread. Bass is also among Whitbread's group of seven largest suppliers and interestingly its own brewing, pub and leisure interest means that it is at once a supplier, competitor and customer of the Whitbread group. Nevertheless, Bass is also working towards full CMI supplier status with Whitbread. The remaining core suppliers were expected to be fully involved by June 1998. Aligning its core suppliers of drinks for resale was Whitbread's top priority, but the company is also investigating the possibility of extending the CMI program to include suppliers of raw materials, bumping the number of CMI suppliers up eventually to around a dozen. In the meantime, in the interests of efficiency, EDI links were extended to a further 32 suppliers during 1997.

Questions for discussion

1. What did Whitbread do to reduce stock holdings within its own distribution network?
2. Under the pilot program of CMI, what benefits do Whitbread and Anheuser have respectively?
3. Based on this case study, please discuss on what factors are the most important ones for the inventory management of beer companies.

New specialized terms

1. high-street off-licenses   商业街上的酒类外卖店
2. grocery multiples   连锁店
3. Co-Managed Inventory (CMI)   共同管理存货
4. SKU (stock-keeping unit)   存储单元
5. stock-out   缺货
6. prime-time overnight delivery slot   高峰期隔夜交付货位
7. back-loading vehicle   装载回程货的车辆

Case summary

Whitbread 啤酒公司的 CMI 方案实施

　　Whitbread 啤酒公司是集酿酒、休闲、饮料零售业务于一体的 Whitbread 集团的酿造分部。Whitbread 集团是英国领先的酿酒商之一，业务领域涉及酒吧、饭店、旅馆，拥有全国最多的商业街上的酒类外卖店。根据 1992 年垄断和兼并委员会颁布的"啤酒法令"，公司的酿酒利润与广域的在线零售利润正式分开。然而，该啤酒公司继续管理着对 Whitbread 集团的线上线下零售网络和其他第三方零售商（主要是大的连锁杂货店）的自产啤酒与第三方制造的饮品供应。

　　市场需求的不断变化，要求 Whitbread 啤酒公司生产多样化产品，但站在酿酒业制造方的角度上，新品牌的大量涌现会使习惯于大批量经营的酿造业管理变得复杂化。生产优化的压力容易导致高的产成品库存，这给管理这些分散在广泛分销系统的产成品带来了困难。这样又反过来危及产品质量，影响保质期，尤其是对那些销量低的高端品牌。

　　20 世纪 90 年代早期，Whitbread 公司着手重组与优化饮品的物流结构，开发更高效、更灵活的网络，以尽可能整合自己的产品库存并向上游供应链渗透。与此同时，上至集团的制造方，下至酒吧、旅馆、商店都引入及时配送模式。在 1995 年，实体店啤酒价格的下滑促使 Whitbread 啤酒公司研究进一步降低其分销网络存货成本的可能性，这可以通过引导主要的第三方零售饮品供应商加入联合管理库存（CMI）协议来实现。CMI 能减少 Whitbread 公司压力，在提高供应能力的同时还能带来备货期与订单周期的根本性缩短。

　　Whitbread 与其最大的线下供应商 Anheuser 公司拉开了协议的序幕。Anheuser 公司是国际酿酒业的巨头、美国酿酒业的老大，占了美国市场份额的 45%，该公司"以最低的库存运送新鲜产品"享誉业界。Anheuser 在英国最大的客户是 Whitbread，其 4 类产品占了 Whitbread 9% 的网下销售量。因此，合作会给双方带来巨大利益。Anheuser 的专长和其相对可预测的交易量使它成为 Whitbread 的理想合作伙伴。两家公司为实施此协议方案而采用了 EDI 技术，系统的供应商是 GE 的信息服务公司。

　　在这一先导方案下，Whitbread 配合 Anheuser 配送中心每日更新的数据，提供 13 周的需求滚动预测值，以通知 Anheuser 计划销售什么和每天已经卖出了什么。Anheuser 据此决定送货的数量和产品组合，来确保库存维持在预订的 2~4 天内并与总体的产品组合相一致。这种灵活操作使供应商能最高效率地管理其生产和运输计划。

　　这一方案将 Whitbread 持有 Anheuser 的产品库存的时间从 8 天降到 4 天，而服务水平从 98.6% 提高到 99.3%。Whitbread 出炉了一系列替代产品，客观上激励 Anheuser 杜绝缺货现象。虽然存货转到了供应商，但是系统总体的存货水平在降低。Anheuser 受益于更准确的销售信息与预测以及更好的资产利用。作为 CMI 的供应商，Anheuser 还能优先获取高峰期隔夜交付货位及允许混合组配的整车运输便利。运输的规律与均衡能够充分利用返程车辆，进一步提高了运输效率。因此，Anheuser 在 1996 年 3 月实现了业务的全面复苏。

1996 年 7 月，Whitbread 与 72 家供应商中的前 7 家供应商召开供应商会议，分享先导 CMI 方案的经验并讨论方案的扩展。数量只占 10%的供应商占到 Whitbread 存货成本的 50%、销售量的 60%、销售金额的 80%。Whitbread 估计，如果把 CMI 方案推广到另外的 6 家供应商，会一次性节约 140 万英镑的成本。进一步讲，更低的存货意味着小的储存场所、更少的分销中心，实现长期成本的大量节约。

1996 年底，Whitbread 的另外两家主要供应商也与 Anheuser 一起加入了 CMI。Bass 位列前七，由于它本身也经营酿造、酒吧娱乐业，这就意味着 Bass 同时是 Whitbread 的供应商、竞争对手和顾客。其余的主要供应商预计将于 1998 年 6 月前全面加入 CMI。Whitbread 虽然最看重联合其核心饮料供应商做分销，但是也在研究将 CMI 项目的合作方扩大到原材料供应商，最终使 CMI 合作供应商达到 12 家。与此同时，为了提高效率，整个 1997 年实现 EDI 链接的供应商已经扩大到 32 家。

▶ Hint for analysis and Reference answer

1. What did Whitbread do to reduce stock holdings within its own distribution network?

In 1995, Whitbread signed CMI agreements with its major third-party suppliers of drinks for the purpose of improving stock availability and affecting a top-change in lead-time and order cycle reduction.

2. Under the pilot program of CMI, what benefits do Whitbread and Anheuser have respectively?

Under the pilot program of CMI, Whitbread's stock of Anheuser products had been reduced from 8 to 4 days, while service levels rose from 98.6 percent to 99.3 percent. Though some inventory was displaced to Anheuser, inventory levels within the system as a whole were reduced. Anheuser benefited from access to better forecasting and sales information, and better utilization of assets. As a CMI supplier it received preferential treatment in the allocation of prime-time overnight delivery slots and was allowed to deliver mixed consignments in full truck-loads. Anheuser's transport efficiencies were further realized by back-loading vehicles.

3. Based on this case study, please discuss on what factors are the most important ones for the inventory management of beer companies.

Many factors including customer service level, quality of forecasting and sales data, usage of asset, information system and JIT transportation and delivery system impact the inventory management of beer companies. Among them, information system and information sharing is the most important one.

Case 11

Healthy & handsome Trading

Healthy & handsome Trading Inc. (HT) has been the sole distributor for Bald and Beauty Hair Products for the past five years. With a strong reputation for high quality, Bald and Beauty's products include dyes, hair permanent kits, lotions, hair curlers, shampoos, hair conditioners, hairstyling sprays, hairbrushes, and combs.

Bald and Beauty's clients consist primarily of major hair salons and pharmacies. HT does not perform the advertising and/or promotion functions for Bald and Beauty. These functions are performed primarily by Bald and Beauty's regional office.

HT manages Bald and Beauty's logistics functions. These functions include inventory management, distribution, and customer service. Bald and Beauty's head office continuously monitors HT's performance. In addition, Bald and Beauty reviews and renegotiates their **third-party distribution contract**[1] every three years.

HT has a small office and distribution center (DC) in a large industrial park in the Midwest. The DC is a two-story facility. The first floor is 900 square feet of storage space, and the second floor is office space. Orders flow into the office by internet from all over the United States. Warehouse workers pick and pack these orders to deliver to the hair salons and pharmacies.

Among Bald and Beauty's products, the Restore Hairdye has been the subject of much management attention recently. Restore Hairdye has a range of twenty-three colors from silvery white to deepest black with wide variations in demand. Some fast-moving colors have stocked out while **slower-moving lines**[2] such as lime green have been on the shelves for up to nine months.

The Restore Hairdye product line has traditionally been a low-cost, high-quality product for Bald and Beauty. However, with competitors recently cutting prices, product substitutes by L'Oreal and other manufacturers have heightened competition and reduced Bald and Beauty's market share. The market is becoming less brand conscious, and with adequate substitute products available, customers are less willing to wait for backorders to be filled.

Bald and Beauty's regional office is aware of the recent drop in market share through regular sales audits. It is also aware of the stockouts, which it feels have led to **brand**

switching[3]. The management of Bald and Beauty has recently pointed out to HT that the number of stockouts has been "alarmingly high" and must be improved. Bald and Beauty issued a written statement to HT, warning that service levels must be drastically improved or HT risks losing the distribution rights when Bald and Beauty reviews its external providers next year.

HT's managing director, Dr. Hank, has called an urgent meeting with Justin, the distribution manager, to discuss the problem.

Conference room conversation

Dr. Hank: What can you tell me about this stockout problem, Justin?

Justin: First, we only experience stockouts with certain colors and at different times. Do you remember the craze for Brute Brown starting about ten months ago? The product was flowing out of the DC like water, and we had many initial stockouts; however, we are on top of that situation now. Several product delays from various suppliers have also contributed to the problem. Copper Brown has been out of stock for a week now due to long lead times. Salons are also constantly dropping brands, changing their orders, and switching orders at the last minute. I think these problems need to be taken up with other areas in the head office, not just the DC staff.

Dr. Hank: Well, I'll speak to the head office about some of these issues. However, we must do whatever is in our control to fix some of these problems immediately. Bald and Beauty requires a very high service level. I've read their policy statements, and they claim they can deliver "above a 90 percent service level." If we want to continue as the logistics provider for Bald and Beauty, we'll have to make their goal ours also. Justin, first I want you to identify the fast-moving colors. I want a 98 percent service level for those and maybe 92 to 95 percent for the slow-moving ones. Revise the inventory policy, and I want to know how much to order and when: remember to factor in all the uncertainties as best you can.

Justin ended: OK, I'll gather the past year's data (Table 4-1) and see what I can do to improve the service level.

Table 4-1 Sales, Stock–out and Service Level Information

Number	Types of colors	Sales volume/$	Out of stock (units)	Service level/%
1	brute brown	66,428	7,188	89
2	burned brown	4,092	792	81
3	charcoal brown	2,742	744	73
4	chestnut	5,220	1,260	76
5	copper brown	81,456	7,584	91
6	deepest black	3,708	924	75
7	deepest pink	1,476	336	77
8	dull yellow	876	144	84

continued

Number	Types of colors	Sales volume/$	Out of stock (units)	Service level/%
9	fiery red	1,044	0	100
10	golden blond	1,104	0	100
11	golden brown	104,640	8,400	92
12	grassy green	576	108	81
13	lemon yellow	816	84	90
14	lightest brown	4,632	888	81
15	lime green	480	0	100
16	orange	648	36	94
17	reddish brown	91,812	6,540	93
18	shocking pink	1,716	0	100
19	silvery white	402	60	85
20	sky blue	972	72	93
21	soft black	3,336	1,020	69
22	tint blonde	1,152	0	100
23	vine brown	5,796	972	83

Note: The annual sales are for the year 2006. Average service level for the year is 90.35%.

▶ Questions for discussion

1. What classification models can be used to effectively classify the Restore Hairdye product?
2. Help Justin to make an inventory policy that is beneficial to strike a balance between inventory cost and customer service level.

▶ New specialized terms

1. third-party distribution contract　第三方分销合约
2. slower-moving line　滞销的产品线
3. brand switching　品牌转换

Case summary

健康英俊贸易公司

健康英俊贸易公司（HT）在过去五年中一直是 Bald 和 Beauty Hair Products（简称 Bald 和 Beauty）的唯一经销商。Bald 和 Beauty 享有高品质的良好声誉，其产品包括染料、头发永久套装、乳液、卷发器、洗发水、护发素、发型喷雾剂、发刷和梳子。

Bald 和 Beauty 的客户主要包括美发沙龙和药房。HT 不负责为 Bald 和 Beauty 做广告或者促销。这些业务主要由 Bald 和 Beauty 的区域办事处执行。

HT 负责 Bald 和 Beauty 的物流功能。这些功能包括库存管理、分销和客户服务。Bald 和 Beauty 的总部持续监控 HT 的表现。此外，Bald 和 Beauty 每三年会审查并重新商谈其第三方分销合同。

HT 在中西部的一个大型工业园区设有一个小型办公室和配送中心（DC）。DC 是一个两层楼的设施：一楼是 900 平方英尺的存储空间，二楼是办公场所。从美国各地的订单通过互联网进入办公室。仓库工人拣选这些订单，派送到美发沙龙和药房。

在 Bald 和 Beauty 的产品中，Restore Hairdye 最近成为管理层关注的焦点。Restore Hairdye 有 23 种颜色，从银白色到最深的黑色，需求变化很大。一些快销的颜色已经被抢购一空，而像石灰绿这样的一些慢销品却已经积存了 9 个月。

Restore Hairdye 生产线传统上一直是 Bald 和 Beauty 的低成本、高品质的产品。然而，随着竞争对手降价，最近欧莱雅和其他制造商的替代品加剧了竞争并降低了 Bald 和 Beauty 的市场份额。市场的品牌意识越来越薄弱，并且有足够的替代产品，客户不太愿意延期交货。

Bald 和 Beauty 的地区办事处通过定期销售审计了解到了最近市场份额的下降，也意识到了产品脱销会导致顾客的品牌转移。Bald 和 Beauty 的管理部门最近向 HT 指出，缺货数量"高得吓人"，必须加以改进。Bald 和 Beauty 向 HT 发出书面声明，警告说，必须大幅提升服务水平，否则当 Bald 和 Beauty 明年对其外部供应商进行评估时，HT 可能会失去分销权。

HT 的总经理汉克博士已召集紧急会议，与分销经理贾斯汀讨论这个问题。下面是他们的对话。

汉克博士：贾斯汀，你能告诉我这个缺货问题吗？

贾斯汀：首先，我们只有在不同的时间上，有特定的颜色缺货。你还记得大约十个月前从 Brute Brown（一种颜色的染发剂）开始的热潮吗？产品像水一样流出 DC，起初我们特别缺货；好在我们已经掌控了局势。来自不同供应商的几次产品延误也导致了这个问题。由于交货时间较长，棕铜色的货已经缺货一周了。此外，美发沙龙不断舍弃品牌，改变订单，并在最后一刻切换订单。我认为这些问题需要总公司的其他部门一起来解决，而不仅仅是 DC 的人员。

汉克博士：嗯，我会和总公司谈谈其中的一些问题。但是，我们必须尽我们所能立即解决其中的一些问题。Bald 和 Beauty 需要非常高的服务水平。我已经看过他们的政策声明，他们声称可以提供"超过 90% 的服务水平"。如果我们想继续作为 Bald 和 Beauty 的物流供应商，我们就必须把他们的目标变成我们的目标。贾斯汀，首先我要你识别最畅销的颜色，我想要为这些品类提供 98% 的服务；对于销售较慢的产品，可能需要提供 92% 到 95% 的服务。请修改库存政策，我想知道订购多少以及什么时候订购，记得尽可能地考虑所有不确定因素。

贾斯汀最后回应：好的，我将收集过去一年的数据，看看我能采取什么措施以提高服务水平。

▷ Hint for analysis and Reference answer

1. What classification models can be used to effectively classify the Restore Hairdye product?

ABC analysis can be applied to classify all the Restore Hairdye product types and CVA (critical value analysis) can be applied to classify the "C" products based on stockout rates.

2. Help Justin to make an inventory policy that is beneficial to striking a balance between inventory cost and customer service level.

Firstly, based on ABC analysis toward 23 Restore Hairdye product types (Table 4-1), Justin should pay utmost attention to the inventory management of "A" color type product containing No.11, No.5, No.1, No.17 in order to raise the average customer service level to over 98%; Next group that should be given priority is "B" color type product containing No. 4, No.23, No.14, No.2, No.6, No.21.

Secondly, applying fixed-order-quantity system for the inventory control of A product and B product while applying fixed-order-interval system for the inventory control of C product.

Case 12

Freshy company

The Freshy company has a logistics department that provides warehousing services to its own retail outlets. Product managers are charged a "warehouse usage fee" according to the percentage of total space in the warehouse their products take up. Freshy uses a product recognition report that gives the net profit for each product. The statement shows sales generated by the product and deducts expenses like manufacturing, distribution, and marketing.

Both executive and product managers use the information from the statement to help them in strategic planning. A regularly occurring strategic issue is which product lines to expand and which lines to drop. Top management develops new business plans based on recommendations from the **strategic planning committee**[1].

A significant cost category in the statement is warehousing. These costs come from storing the product after it leaves the manufacturing facility but before it arrives at the retail outlet. Typical warehousing costs include labor, material handling equipment, and **depreciation on the warehouse**[2].

The warehouse has 60,000 cubic feet, which costs the firm 60,000 dollars, annually. Freshy company has three categories of products, knowing as X, Y and Z. Product X (steel tire rims) takes up one-sixth of the warehouse space, so it is allocated $10,000 ($60,000 total cost times 10,000 cubic feet used by Product X divided by 60,000 total warehouse space). Product Y (consumer electronics) takes up one-third of the warehouse space, so it is allocated $20,000 ($60,000 total cost times 20,000 cubic feet used by Product Y divided by 60,000 total warehouse space). Product Z (pillows) takes up one-half of the warehouse space, so it is allocated $30,000 ($60,000 total cost times 30,000 cubic feet used by Product Z divided by 60,000 total warehouse space).

Wendy, manager of product Z, receive a product recognition report that shows a negative profit for her product line. She realizes that the product may be discontinued. When the vice president of sales asks her to defend product Z, Wendy explains that the current **accounting method**[3] allocates too much of the warehouse cost to her product line.

Wendy argues that while pillows takes up fifty percent of the warehouse space, most of the warehouse costs come from material handling. Wendy further argues that pillows are the easiest of the three products to handle, so they should be allocated a smaller portion of the warehousing costs. She believes that the other two products should be allocated more warehousing costs because they are harder to handle than pillows. Wendy is told, "Sorry, this is the way costs are allocated."

Wendy has a couple of complaints. First, she feels that incorrect accounting techniques make her product's performance look poor. Furthermore, Wendy believes that by allocating fixed cost to products, upper-level managers are basing their decisions partly on irrelevant data. She receives permission from the vice president of finance/accounting to hire you as a consultant to see if the company needs to change its accounting system to make it more accurately reflect the costs associated with each product line.

▶ Questions for discussion

1. What do you think of Wendy's arguments regarding the current accounting system?
2. What suggestions and rationale should be included in your report to the vice president?

▶ New specialized terms

1. strategic planning committee   战略规划委员会
2. depreciation on the warehouse   仓库折旧
3. accounting method   会计核算方法

Case summary

新 鲜 公 司

新鲜公司下设一个物流部,旨在为自营的零售店提供仓储服务。各类产品则根据它们占用仓库空间的百分比来收取"仓库使用费"。新鲜公司通过产品识别报告计算出每种产品的净利润,报表显示了该产品的销售额以及扣除掉的制造、分销和营销等费用。

公司高管和产品经理都使用报表中的信息来帮助他们进行战略规划。一个经常出现的战略问题是哪些产品线要扩展,哪些产品线要终止。最高管理层在战略规划委员会建议的基础上制订新的商业计划。

报表中的一个重要成本类别是仓储。这些成本来自产品出厂与运抵零售店之前的存储环节。典型的仓储成本包括人工、物料搬运设备和仓库折旧。

仓库有 60 000 立方英尺,每年花费 60 000 美元。新鲜公司有三类产品,分别为 X、Y、Z。产品 X(钢轮辋)占据仓库空间的 1/6,因此分配给它 10 000 美元(总产品成本为 60 000 美元乘以产品占用的 10 000 立方英尺除以 60 000 总仓库空间)。产品 Y(消费类电子产品）占据仓库空间的 1/3，因此分配 20 000 美元（总产品成本为 60 000 美元乘以产品 Y 占用的 20 000 立方英尺除以 60 000 总仓库空间）。产品 Z（枕头）占据仓库空间的一半，因此分配 30 000 美元（60 000 美元的总成本乘以产品 Z 使用的 30 000 立方英尺除以 60 000 总仓库空间）。

产品 Z 的经理 Wendy 收到产品识别报告，显示 Z 产品线的利润为负。她意识到该产品可能会停产。当销售副总裁征求 Wendy 对产品 Z 的辩护时，Wendy 解释说，目前的会计方法将过多的仓库成本分配给她的产品线。

Wendy 认为，虽然枕头占据了 50%的仓库空间，但大部分仓库成本来自物料处理。Wendy 进一步辩称，枕头是三种产品中最容易处理的，因此它们应分摊更少的仓储成本。她认为另外两种产品应分摊更多的仓储成本，因为它们比枕头更难处理。Wendy 收到的答复是："对不起，这就是分配成本的方式。"

Wendy 为此产生了若干抱怨。首先，她认为不正确的核算方法导致她的产品绩效看起来很差。此外，Wendy 认为，通过将固定成本分配给各类产品，高层管理者的决策在一定程度上是基于不相关的数据。她从财务/会计副总裁那里获得了许可，聘请你来当顾问，以考察该公司是否需要更改会计制度，以便更准确地反映与每个产品线相关的成本。

Hint for analysis and Reference answer

1. What do you think of Wendy's arguments regarding the current accounting system?

Wendy's arguments regarding the current accounting system is reasonable.

Both handling and holding cost of steel tire rims and consumer electronics are larger than that of pillows. The current accounting system is a kind of traditional method in allocating mixed costs, which is not beneficial to clarifying cost and exacting responsibility in cost control.

2. What suggestions and rationale should be included in your report to the vice president?

Firstly, upper-level managers should base their decisions on relevant data; Secondly, accounting managers should develop information about cost drivers and resulting causal relationships and allocating indirect expenses based on labor, material handling and depreciation rather than only on warehouse space.

Part Five

Logistics Information Management

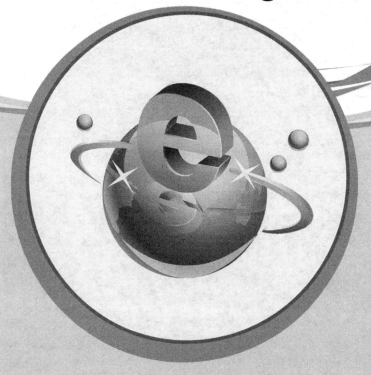

Part Five Logistics Information Management

Learning Objectives

After learning this part, you will be able to:
- Understand the importance of information and information technology in a supply chain
- Identify the strategies, and the technologies used to give a firm's manufacturing and logistics operations a huge competitive edge
- Assess different types of information in integrated logistics system
- Understand how the application of technology to data collection and analysis allows a company to spot trends and gain insight into the future preferences of customers

Case 13

Care-free Hut

Care-free Hut is a small, independent supermarket operating in a suburb of Houston. The shop has managed to maintain profitability over the past twenty years. The nearest competition comes from a large national retailer which is located five miles away (15 minutes away by car). Care-free Hut has relatively high margin and is conveniently located for the surrounding medium to high density community.

The shop consists of a small building equally divided between the retail/display section and the warehousing section. The warehouse is at the rear of the building and is used to store safety stock. Each week Jay Reid, the manager/owner of Care-free Hut, walks through the store, examine the shelves, and determines which items are low or out of stock. After determining the current status of stock on the shelves and allowing for safety stock already on the premises, Jay places replenishment orders. Jay bases the quantity to order on his own estimate of demand for each item, taking into account the minimum size of each orders. Due to the relatively slow turnover and small size of the shop, Jay limits the variety to one brand per product.

Jay has just learned that a property developer is demolishing the abandoned power station nearby and will build a large retail complex just around the corner from Care-free Hut. Jay has also discovered from the local city council that a major tenant of the center, one of the "anchors" will be a store that belongs to a large, **publicly listed supermarket chain**[1].

From his own research, Jay has learned that this new retailer's motto is "higher service, lower prices guaranteed." He has also learned that the company uses principles such as just-in-time inventory control, **centralized warehousing facilities**[2], and **vendor managed inventories**[3]. The retail outlet also makes extensive use of bar coding, especially in inventory management and automated ordering. Inspection of the proposed plans showed that the new store would be seven times the size of Care-free Hut, but would use about the same amount of space for warehousing. Jay's lease is up for renewal at the same time as the proposed opening of the new store. Jay comes to you for assistance since you have a solid understanding of your logistics management.

Jay seeks your advice and an explanation of these new, unknown terms and practices. He also wants to know how the new store could possibly provide high service, low prices, and low stockout rates with such a small storage area.

▶ Questions for discussion

1. Write a report for Jay, explaining each of the new store's inventory management principles and warehousing concepts and how these can be used to achieve lower prices.
2. Offer Jay some suggestions with regard to making Care-free Hut more competitive with the incoming retail supermarket.

▶ New specialized terms

1. publicly listed supermarket chain   上市的连锁超市
2. centralized warehousing facility   集中式的仓储设施
3. vendor managed inventories   卖方管理库存

Case summary

Care-free Hut

Care-free Hut 是一家位于休斯敦郊区的小型独立超市。该店在过去 20 年中一直保持盈利。最近的竞争对手是一家大型的全国性零售商，距离该超市有 5 英里（15 分钟车程）。Care-free Hut 具有相对较高的利润率，位置便利，适合周围的中高密度社区。

该商店由零售/展示区和仓储区之间的小型建筑组成。仓库位于建筑物的后部，用于存放安全库存。Care-free Hut 的经理 Jay Reid 每周去商店检查货架，并确定哪些商品存量少或缺货。在确定货架上的当前库存状态以及允许的在库安全库存后，Jay 再下补货订单。Jay 考虑到每次订单的最小规模，根据他自己对每个项目的需求估计来确定实际订货量。

由于店铺规模较小且周转相对较慢，Jay 将每种产品的品种限制为一个品牌。

Jay 刚刚得知一家房地产开发商正在拆除附近废弃的发电站，并将在 Care-free Hut 的对角建造一个大型零售综合体。Jay 还从当地市政厅了解到，该中心的主要租户将是属于大型上市连锁超市的支柱门店之一。

根据自己的研究，Jay 了解到这个新零售商的座右铭是"更高的服务，更低的价格保证"。他还了解到公司奉行的原则包括即时库存控制、集中式的仓储设施和卖方管理库存。零售店还广泛使用条形码，特别是在库存管理和自动订购方面。通过审视计划得知，新店的面积是 Care-free Hut 的 7 倍，但是用于仓储的空间大致相同。在那家新店行将开张的同时，Jay 的店铺也将面临续租。

鉴于您对物流管理很内行，Jay 现在寻求您的建议，并希望能够理解新的、未知的术语或做法。他还想知道新店如何能够在如此小的存储空间下提供高质量服务并实现低价格和低缺货率。

Hint for analysis and Reference answer

1. Write a report for Jay, explaining each of the new store's inventory management principles and warehousing concepts and how these can be used to achieve lower prices.

The inventory management principles used by the new store include just-in-time inventory control, centralized warehousing facilities, and vendor managed inventories.

Just-in-time inventory control is an inventory management strategy that is aimed at monitoring the inventory process in such a manner as to minimize the costs associated with inventory control and maintenance. To a great degree, a just-in-time inventory process relies on the efficient monitoring of the usage of materials in the production of goods and ordering replacement goods that arrive shortly before they are needed.

Centralizing warehousing is a system where a retailer maintains a single, central warehouse versus several facilities spread out to cover a territory. Compared to decentralized warehousing, a centralized approach may offer a number of benefits, such as better customer service, lower operation costs and lower inbound costs.

Vendor managed inventory (VMI) is an inventory management technique in which a supplier of goods is responsible for optimizing the inventory held by a distributor. The benefits of a VMI system may include better inventory accuracy, forecasting, and service, though it can present challenges in communication and cultural resistance.

A warehouse serves as a transportation consolidation facility, acts as a reservoir for production overflow, and is the sites for product mixing and production facilitators. Above all, it can provide good customer service.

2. Offer Jay some suggestions with regard to making Care-free Hut more competitive with the incoming retail supermarket.

Jay should first make full use of advanced information technologies such as RFID, EDI, CPFR and CRM to improve the Hut's warehousing efficiency. Then he should strengthen systematic operational information exchange with his suppliers and customers. Moreover, building strong corporate culture and empowering front-line employees more rights to serve customers are also very important to enhance the Hut's competitiveness.

Case 14

WorthPal Inc.

In the late 1990s, Loren Inc. had sales slightly over $75 million. The firm was located in the Midwest and was involved in supplying automotive manufacturers with tires, brake drums, and batteries. Logistics costs accounted for about 30% of sales. More specifically, transportation costs were $11 million, warehousing costs totaled $2.5 million, and inventory costs were approximately $7 million. The rest of the logistics costs came from order processing, material handling and packaging, and totaled about $2 million.

Loren had four warehouses, one private and on site, the others public and located within 100 miles of the plant. The firm had contracts with six carriers to bring material inbound and finished goods outbound to its customers. In recent years, Loren's customers had pressured it into a **JIT delivery system**[1], which in turn forced Loren into a JIT manufacturing environment. Becoming a JIT manufacturer required Loren to use carriers that could fulfill its JIT demands for inbound and outbound delivery. **Inbound truckload shipments**[2] totaled over 150 trailer loads monthly, and outbound totaled almost 100 loads monthly. Loren was located perfectly for JIT because its plants and warehouses were no more than 350 miles (one day by truck) from its clients. In turn, all of Loren's carriers were no more than 600 miles (two days by truck) from Loren's plant and all four warehouses.

Of Loren's six carriers, WorthPal was considered the most dependable and reliable. However, WorthPal was the smallest of Loren's carriers, with twenty of its thirty-five tractor trailers dedicated to Loren's freight. It was under contract with Loren for a little less than $3 million in annual revenue. Loren was WorthPal's largest client, accounting for about 40% of revenue. In total, WorthPal's annual revenue was around $7.5 million. It had become dependent on Loren for business.

Loren determined that all of its carriers must have EDI systems and automated tracking capabilities. Furthermore, documentation and billing procedures could be handled over the computer, increasing efficiency and reducing cost. In this manner, Loren could ensure that its carriers met delivery schedules. If a shipment was late, loren could contact the carrier immediately, trace the shipment, and found out when it would arrive, not only did the **electronic documentation flow**[3] increase efficiencies and reduce cost, it also allowed for fewer mistakes and better control over freight movements. Another requirement was that each carrier dedicate equipment to Loren. All of loren's carriers had their required EDI systems in place except WorthPal, and all carriers were willing to dedicate equipment for Loren.

WorthPal found that it would take nearly $1 million to install computers in its truck cabs and implement EDI with Loren. WorthPal lacked the cash flow to do this and could not borrow from the bank. Therefore, WorthPal told Loren that it could not meet its requirements. This decision was extremely difficult to make because WorthPal knew that losing 40% of its business would probably force it into bankruptcy.

Upon hearing of WorthPal's decision, Loren' s management was visibly upset. WorthPal had provided quality transportation service to Loren for over four years, and the two companies had developed a very strong and successful working relationship. To continue WorthPal's service, Loren proposed to invest in EDI for WorthPal if it would give Loren an additional 25% discount on rates once the system was up and running. Loren calculated that it would take six months to install the EDI system and two years to regain the investment. This was a small price to pay to ensure that its best carrier would continue service. And down the road, the additional 25% discount cold reap many financial returns. As part of the package, Loren guaranteed WorthPal that freight volume would increase. WorthPal's management hesitated because of the discount. This would reduce its revenue by $750,000 annually, making **positive cash flow**[4] difficult. But what choice did it have? The outlook for more volume from Loren might offset the short-term drop in revenue, and having the EDI system could bring additional business into the firm in the form of other clients. WorthPal reluctantly agreed to Loren's terms.

Questions for discussion

1. What is your opinion of Loren's decision to help WorthPal?
2. What do you think of WorthPal' decision to accept Loren's offer?
3. What benefits could WorthPal and Loren realize besides avoiding bankruptcy and lowering transportation rates?

New specialized terms

1. JIT delivery system   准时制交付（送货）系统
2. inbound truckload shipment   输入的整车运输量
3. electronic documentation flow   电子单证流
4. positive cash flow   正的现金流

Case summary

WorthPal 公司

在 20 世纪 90 年代末期，Loren 公司的销售额略高于 7 500 万美元。该公司位于中西部，为汽车制造商提供轮胎、制动鼓和电池，物流成本约占销售额的 30%，具体地讲，运输成本为 1 100 万美元；仓储成本总计 250 万美元，库存成本约为 700 万美元。其余的物流成本来自订单处理、物料处理和包装，总计约 200 万美元。

Loren 有四个仓库，一个是自建仓库（设在公司内部），其余是公共仓库，距离工厂 100 英里。该公司与 6 家运输商签订了合同，负责将原材料输入厂内和成品输出给客户。近年来，Loren 的客户迫使其实施准时交付系统，这使 Loren 不得不引入准时制造体系，这要求 Loren 聘用的运输商能满足输入交付与输出交付的准时要求。输入的整车装运量每月总计超过 150 个拖车，输出的装运量每月总计近 100 个拖车。Loren 的位置是极其适应准时制的，因为它的工厂和仓库距离客户不超过卡车一天的路程（350 英里），因此 Loren 的所有运输商距离 Loren 的工厂和所有 4 个仓库都不超过卡车两天的路程（600 英里）。

在 Loren 的 6 家运输商中，WorthPal 是最可靠的，但也是规模最小的，其 35 辆拖挂车中有 20 辆专门用于 Loren 的货运。WorthPal 与 Loren 签订了年收入不到 300 万美元的合同，Loren 是 WorthPal 最大的客户，占其收入的 40% 左右。WorthPal 的年收入约为 750 万美元，已然在业务上对 Loren 形成了依赖。

Loren 决定让其所有运输商必须拥有 EDI 系统并能实现自动跟踪功能，单证与计费程序也要通过计算机，以便提高效率并降低成本。通过这种方式，Loren 才可以确保其运输商达到交付时间的要求。如果发货延迟，Loren 可以立即联系承运商跟踪货物，搞清楚何时能送达。单证电子化不仅提高了效率、降低了成本，还减少了错误并更好地控制货运。另一个要求是每个运输商都将设备专用于 Loren，除 WorthPal 之外，所有 Loren 的运输商都拥有所需的 EDI 系统，所有运输商都愿意为 Loren 投入专用设备。

WorthPal 发现在卡车驾驶室安装计算机并与 Loren 实施电子数据交换需要花费近 100 万美元，但目前没有现金来做这件事，也无法向银行借款。因此，WorthPal 通知 Loren 它无法满足其要求。这是个艰难的抉择，因为 WorthPal 知道失去 40% 的业务可能会迫使它破产。

得知 WorthPal 的决定后，Loren 的管理层明显感到失望。WorthPal 已经为 Loren 提供了超过 4 年的优质运输服务，两家公司已经建立了良好的关系。为了延续 WorthPal 的服务，Loren 考虑投资建设 WorthPal 的电子数据交换系统，前提是，一旦系统启动并运行，WorthPal 将给 Loren 额外的 25% 的费用折扣（作为补偿）。Loren 核算后得知，安装 EDI 系统需要 6 个月，回收投资需要两年时间。相较于确保其最好的运输商继续为之服务，这是一个很小的代价。额外的 25% 折扣也可带来许多财务收益。作为一揽子计划的一部分，

Loren 保证 WorthPal 承担的货运量将增加。但由于存在运价折扣条款，WorthPal 的管理层犹豫不决。这将使其每年收入减少 75 万美元，从而实现正的现金流变得困难。但它还有什么其他选择吗？来自 Loren 的更多业务量预期有可能抵消短期的收入下降，而拥有电子数据交换系统可能会吸引其他客户为 WorthPal 带来额外的业务。WorthPal 勉强地接受了 Loren 的条款。

Hint for analysis and Reference answer

1. What is your opinion of Loren's decision to help WorthPal?

Loren's decision to help WorthPal is wise since in the long-run, Loren can reap many financial returns with only a small price to pay.

2. What do you think of WorthPal' decision to accept Loren's offer?

WorthPal' decision to accept Loren's offer is also reasonable because the deal between them is a win-win game.

3. What benefits could WorthPal and Loren realize besides avoiding bankruptcy and lowering transportation rates?

WorthPal and Loren can realize many benefits through such a collaboration on implementing EDI.

EDI solutions are perfect for seamless integration into a supply chain system because of better information flows between involved partners. EDI significantly reduces administrative, maintenance, and resource costs due to transactions automation and less involvement of paper usage. EDI also enlarges both companies' customer base and efficiently managing trade partner relationship owing to its quicker goods and services distribution.

Case 15

Supply-Base Reduction at Rabbity

On May 18, 2004, Robert Ryan met with John Lucas, purchasing director of Rabbity Corporation at Rabbity's corporate headquarters in Phoenix, Arizona. "Your new assignment, as part of your recent transfer to the strategic sourcing manager position, is to make recommendations on how best to utilize information technology in our chassis and body parts supply-base reduction efforts. I expect your recommendations in 2 months," John said.

Company Background

Rabbity Corporation operates a fleet of nearly 30,000 trucks, one of the largest fleets in North America. The company provides transportation services to more than 25 million residential, municipal, and industrial customers across North America. With more than 1,200 locations have dealt with thousands of different parts suppliers across the country using separate legacy systems. Rabbity is currently in the process of moving toward **centralized strategy development**[1] and price negotiation, but will still have **decentralized order execution**[2]. On the corporate level, Rabbity now has 10 strategic sourcing teams working closely with employees throughout the company to define needs, find the best suppliers, and develop systems for streamlined purchasing.

One of the key points of Rabbity's **overall business strategy**[3] involves implementing a procurement process that will leverage the company's size to realize savings and discounts through consolidation and reduction of the number of suppliers used by reducing the number of suppliers to ensure low prices, high quality, timely delivery, excellent customer service, and strong buyer-supplier relationships.

Chassis and Body Parts Project

One specific supply-base reduction project that Rabbity has recently undertaken involves chassis and body part purchases for their fleet of trucks. Chassis and body parts were selected for supply-base reduction efforts because the supply base was highly fragmented, the purchase volumes were not leveraged, there was no centralized purchasing process, this was a large area of spend that provided a good opportunity for savings, and because opportunities for product and information technology standardization existed. Currently, Rabbity purchases chassis and body parts from over 15,000 suppliers. Rabbity would like to create a preferred supplier list of

6 chassis parts suppliers and 6 body parts suppliers.

Nature of Supply Market

The supply market for vehicle parts is comprised of many suppliers in a highly competitive struggle to earn customers. The products are readily available from many sources and supplier location has traditionally been an important selection criterion.

Questions for discussion

1. What types of information technologies might be useful in Rabbity's supply-base reduction efforts?
2. What recommendations would you make to Robert Ryan?
3. How might reducing the number of suppliers facilitate the additional use of information technology and additional information sharing?
4. What problems or challenges might Rabbity face as it implements these technologies?

New specialized terms

1. centralized strategy development 集权式战略制定
2. decentralized order execution 分权式订单执行
3. overall business strategy 总体经营战略

Case summary

Rabbity 公司的供应基地缩减

2004年5月18日，总部位于亚利桑那州凤凰城的 Rabbity 公司采购经理 John Lucas 会见了 Robert Ryan，并任命后者为战略采购主管，要求在两个月内，本着减少成本的目的，提出关于如何最佳地利用信息技术努力减少底盘和车身部件供应基地的建议书。

Rabbity 公司是北美最大的运输队之一，拥有3万辆卡车，为北美2500万居民、政府、企业服务。全国1200个服务点用单独的现存系统应对全国各地的成千上万的部件供应商。当前，Rabbity 正在转向集权化战略开发和价格协商，但其订单执行仍是分权化的。Rabbity 公司的集团层拥有10个战略采购团队，他们与全公司员工密切合作以界定需要、寻找最佳供应商和研发精益采购系统。

Rabbity 公司总体运营战略的关键点之一是实施一种采购过程，使公司发挥自身规模的优势，通过整合与减少供应商的数量实现节约、获得折扣，确保低价格、高质量、及时配送、优良的顾客服务水平和稳固的供需关系。

Rabbity 公司近期运作的具体的供应基地缩减项目包括对其成队卡车的底盘和车身部

件的采购。由于供应地分散，未能发挥采购规模优势，没有集中化购买流程，因此这方面存在很大的利用现有信息技术节约开支的机会。当前Rabbity公司从超过15 000家供应商处购买底盘和车身部件，未来打算把底盘供应商与车身部件供应商均缩减到6家。

车辆零部件市场由许多供应商组成，为争夺顾客的竞争十分激烈。产品可从许多渠道获得，而供应商的位置历来是一项重要的选择标准。

▶ Hint for analysis and Reference answer

1. What types of information technologies might be useful in Rabbity's supply-base reduction efforts?

Information technologies like MRP, ERP, JIT, CPR, VMI, ECM(企业商务管理) might be useful.

2. What recommendations would you make to Robert Ryan?

Firstly, optimize Rabbity's purchasing process to make it achieve cost saving and good service based on economies of scale.

Secondly, focus on forging strategic partnerships with the few suppliers remained, pay more attention to the continuity of relationship, mutual trust and creating loyalty.

Thirdly, strive to realize systematic operational information exchange with key suppliers.

3. How might reducing the number of suppliers facilitate the additional use of information technology and additional information sharing?

A firm's information system can be effective and lead to active information sharing only through sound relationship with its partners, while close relationships can be maintained with only a few suppliers.

4. What problems or challenges might Rabbity face as it implements these technologies?

Possible problems or challenges are weak power, fragile relations, crisis of trust, safety concern, too much information, lack of standard, inaccurate information, and etc.

Case 16

Enterprise-Level Coordination at Zappos

Tony Hsieh's first entrepreneurial effort began at the age of 12 when he started his own custom button business. Realizing the importance of advertising, Hsieh began marketing his business to other kids through directories, and soon his profits soared to a few hundred dollars a month. Throughout his adolescence, Hsieh started several businesses, and by the time he was in college he was making money selling pizzas out of his Harvard dorm room. Another entrepreneurial student, Alfred Lin, bought pizzas from Hsieh and resold them by the slice, making a nice profit. Hsieh and Lin quickly became friends.

After Harvard, Hsieh founded LinkExchange in 1996, a company that helped small businesses exchange banner ads. A mere two years later, Hsieh sold LinkExchange to Microsoft for $265 million. Using the profits from the sale, Hsieh and Lin formed a **venture capital company**[1] that invested in **start-up businesses**[2]. One investment that caught their attention was Zappos, an **online etailer**[3] of shoes. Both entrepreneurs viewed the $40 billion shoe market as an opportunity they could not miss, and in 2000 Hsieh took over as Zappos' CEO with Lin as his chief financial officer. Today, Zappos is leading its market and offering an enormous selection of more than 90,000 styles of handbags, clothing, and accessories for more than 500 brands. One reason for Zappos' incredible success was Hsieh's decision to use the advertising and marketing budget for customer service, a tactic that would not have worked before the Internet. Zappos' passionate customer service strategy encourages customers to order as many sizes and styles of products as they want, ships them for free, and offers **free return shipping**[4]. Zappos encourages customer communication, and its call center receives more than 5,000 calls a day with the longest call to date lasting more than four hours. Zappos' extensive inventory is stored in a warehouse in Kentucky right next to a UPS shipping center. Only available stock is listed on the website, and orders as late as 11 P.M. are still guaranteed **next-day delivery**[5]. To facilitate supplier and partner relationships, Zappos built an extranet that provides its vendors with all kinds of product information, such as items sold, times sold, price, customer, and so on. Armed with these kinds of details, suppliers can quickly change manufacturing schedules to meet demand.

Along with valuing its partners and suppliers, Zappos also places a great deal of value on its employee relationships. Zappos' employees have fun, and walking through the offices you will see all kinds of things not normally seen in business environments — bottle-cap pyramids, cotton-candy machines, and bouncing balls. Building loyal employee relationships is a critical success factor at Zappos, and to facilitate this relationship the corporate headquarters are located in the same building as the call center (where most employees work) in Las Vegas. All employees receive 100 percent company-paid health insurance along with a daily free lunch. Of course, the Zappos culture does not work for everyone, and the company pays to find the right employees through "The Offer," which extends to new employees the option of quitting and receiving payment for time worked plus an additional $1,000 bonus. Why the $1,000 bonus for quitting? Zappos' management believes that is a small price to pay to find those employees who do not have the sense of commitment Zappos requires. Less than 10 percent of new hires take "The Offer". Zappos' unique culture stresses the following:

1. Delivering WOW through service
2. Embracing and driving change
3. Creating fun and a little weirdness
4. Being adventurous, creative, and open-minded
5. Pursuing growth and learning
6. Building open and honest relationships with communication
7. Building a positive team and family spirit
8. Doing more with less
9. Being passionate and determined
10. Being humble Zappos' Sale

Amazon.com purchased Zappos for $880 million. Zappos employees shared $40 million in cash and stock, and the Zappos management team remained in place. Having access to Amazon's world-class warehouses and supply chain is sure to catapult Zappos' revenues, though many wonder whether the Zappos culture will remain. It'll be interesting to watch!

▷ Questions for discussion

1. Explain CRM and why Zappos would benefit from the implementation of a CRM system.
2. Why does Zappos emphasize building loyal employee relationships?
3. Analyze the merger between Zappos and Amazon and assess potential issues for Zappos' customers.

▷ New specialized terms

1. venture capital company   风险投资公司
2. start-up business   创业公司

3. online etailer　在线电子零售商
4. free return shipping　免除退货的运费
5. next-day delivery　隔日送达

Case summary

发生在 Zappos 公司的企业之间的协调

Tony Hsieh 十二岁时开始第一次创业，经营定制纽扣业务。后来他认识到了广告的重要性，便开始通过电话号码簿向其他孩子开展营销，每月利润猛增到数百美元。少年时代积累了几次创业经验后，Hsieh 又在就读的哈佛宿舍内销售披萨。此时，另一位创业学生 Alfred Lin 从 Hsieh 处买了比萨后切割销售，也获得了不菲的利润。二人迅速成为朋友。

离开哈佛后，Hsieh 于 1996 年创立了 LinkExchange 公司，旨在帮助小企业交换旗帜广告。仅仅两年后，Hsieh 以 2.65 亿美元将 LinkExchange 卖给了微软公司。通过这笔销售得来的利润，Hsieh 与 Lin 组建了风险投资公司，向初创企业投资。此时，在线鞋类零售商 Zappos 引起了他俩的注意，他们认为必须抓住每年规模高达 400 亿美元的鞋类市场机会。2000 年，Hsieh 与 Lin 分别担任 Zappos 的总裁与首席财务官。如今，Zappos 居于市场领先地位，经营 500 多个品牌，9 万多种款式的手袋、服装与配件。Zappos 取得非凡成功的一个重要原因是 Hsieh 决定将广告与营销预算用到客户服务上，这是互联网时代之前不可能奏效的策略。Zappos 的充满激情的客户服务战略鼓励其客户大批量、多款式订货，免运费，甚至退货产生的运费也不收。Zappos 同时鼓励与客户沟通，其呼叫中心一天能接到 5 000 次电话，迄今最长的一次电话沟通长达 4 个小时。Zappos 的存货设在肯塔基州的仓库，紧邻 UPS 的货运中心。其现有存货数量展示在网站上，截至晚上 11 点的订单都能保证次日送达。为了加强与其供应商与伙伴的关系，Zappos 设计了外网，向供应商提供所有的产品信息，包括已售货品类型、时间、价格等等。有了这些详细信息，供应商们能够迅速改变生产计划以应对需求。

Zappos 在重视供应商与伙伴关系的同时，也十分重视员工关系。Zappos 的员工充满乐趣，走进工作区你常会见到各类在办公场所很难见到的现象，如瓶盖塔、棉花糖机器与弹力球等。建立忠诚的员工关系是 Zappos 成功的关键因素。为拉近与员工的关系，公司总部与员工数量最多的呼叫中心设在拉斯维加斯的同一个楼内。所有员工都享受公司 100%买单的健康保险与免费午餐。由于公司文化不一定适合于每个人，Zappos 拨专款推出一种"Offer"，"奖励"员工的离职，真正目的在于发掘适合的员工。这种"Offer"扩展到了新员工，如果新人离职将可以得到以前工作时段的报酬另加 1 000 美元的奖金。事实上，只有不到 10%的员工得到过这种"Offer"。Zappos 的独特文化强调以下几点：

1. 通过服务传递"惊喜"

2. 拥抱并推动变化
3. 创造乐趣，彰显另类
4. 敢于冒险、创新、开放
5. 追求成长与学习
6. 开诚布公，密切协商
7. 打造积极的团队，倡导"家"的精神
8. 开源节流
9. 有主见、富激情
10. 做低调的 Zappos 销售员

亚马逊以 8.8 亿美元收购了 Zappos，员工分享了 4 000 万美元的现金与股票资产，而 Zappos 的管理团队依然保留。利用亚马逊世界级的仓库与供应链肯定会大幅提升 Zappos 的收入，尽管许多人对 Zappos 文化能否延续持有怀疑。让我们拭目以待吧！

Hint for analysis and Reference answer

1. Explain CRM and why Zappos would benefit from the implementation of a CRM system.

Customer relationship management (CRM) is a strategy for managing a company's interaction with its customers with the goal of improving customer satisfaction, customer retention, and sales growth. A CRM System helps a company in achieving these goals by streamlining communication across different mediums and providing insights about customers to key decision makers in the organization. Customer facing teams such as Sales, Marketing, and Customer Support use a CRM system to communicate with customers, schedule appointments, nurture deals, handle customer complaints, store customer information, and so on.

Zappos would benefit from the implementation of a CRM system because having a good CRM system will increase revenue and support team productivity through better deal nurturing and follow-ups, improve its customer relations, enhance both internal communication and external collaboration with supply chain partners, as well as reduce risks to businesses.

2. Why does Zappos emphasize building loyal employee relationships?

In the new economics of service, frontline employees and customers need to be the center of management concern. Just like the manager of JW Marriott said: "You can't make the guests happy with unhappy employees". Employee satisfaction is of utmost importance for employees to remain happy and also realize their best performance. Satisfied employees are the ones who are extremely loyal towards their organization and stick to it even in the worst scenario. They do not work out of any compulsion but because they dream of taking their organization to a new level. Employees need to be passionate towards their work and passion comes only when employees are satisfied with their job and organization on the whole. Employee satisfaction leads to a positive atmosphere at the workplace. Loyal employee relationships are essential to ensure higher and sustainable revenues for the organization.

3. Analyze the merger between Zappos and Amazon and assess potential issues for Zappos' customers.

The merger between Zappos and Amazon will enlarge Zappos' retail market and boost its revenue in the long run. However, clashes of culture between two companies can occur, reducing the effectiveness of the integration. In addition, such a merger might make some employees redundant, especially at management levels—this may lead to a negative effect on motivation.

Mergers often bring a mixture of welcome and not-so-welcome changes to the workplace. Employee morale drops to an all-time low during a company restructuring during a merger. With the instability of the situation, employees often lose the desire to come to work or to do their best work. The new company might bring a reduction in benefits or employee programs, which further affects morale. Employees of Zappos might become disengaged and disenchanted. Zappos' customers may suffer from low-moral of Zappos' employees.

Part Six

Supply Chain Management

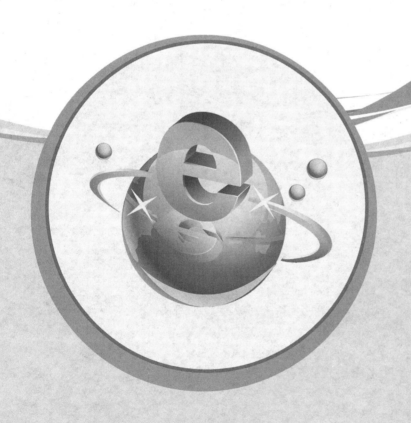

Part Six Supply Chain Management

Learning Objectives

After learning this part, you will be able to:
- Gain an understanding of the characteristics of supply chain management
- Get an overview of supply chain management philosophies, principles and their implications for enterprises
- Devise a supply chain system fit for a manufacturing firm or retailing firm

Case 17

Managing Growth at SportStuff

In December 2000, Sanjay Gupta and his management team were busy evaluating the performance at SportStuff over the last year. Demand had grown by 80 percent over the year. This growth, however, was a mixed blessing. The **venture capitalists**[1] supporting the company were very pleased with the growth in sales and the resulting increase in revenue. Sanjay and his team, however, could clearly see that costs would grow faster than revenues if demand continued to row and the supply chain network was not redesigned. They decided to analyze the performance of the current network to see how it could be redesigned to best cope with the rapid growth anticipated over the next three years.

Sanjay Gupta founded SportStuff in 1996 with a mission of supplying parents with more affordable sports equipment for their children. Parents complained about having to discard expensive skates, skis, jackets, and shoes because children outgrew them rapidly. Sanjay's initial plan was for the company to purchase used equipment and jackets from families and any surplus equipment from manufacturers and retailers and sell these over the Internet. The idea was very well received in the marketplace, demand grew rapidly, and by the end of 1996 the company had sales of $0.8 million. By this time a variety of new and used products were sold and the company received significant venture capital support.

In June 1996, Sanjay leased part of a warehouse in the outskirts of St. Louis to manage the large amount of product being sold. Suppliers sent their product to the warehouse. Customer orders were packed and shipped by UPS from there. As demand grew, SportStuff leased more space within the warehouse. By 1999, SportStuff leased the entire warehouse and shipped to customers all over the United Sates. Management divided the United States into 6 customer zones for planning purposes. Demand for each customer zone in 1999 was shown in Table 6-1. Sanjay estimated that the next three years would see a growth rate of about 80 percent per year, after which demand would **level off**[2]. Sanjay and his management team could see that they needed more warehouse space to cope with the anticipated growth. One option was to lease more warehouse space in St. Louis itself. Other options included leasing warehouses all over the country. Leasing a warehouse involved fixed costs based on the size of the warehouse and variable costs that varied with the quantity shipped through the warehouse. Four potential locations for warehouses were identified in Denver, Seattle, Atlanta, and Philadelphia. Warehouses leased could be either small (about 100,000 sq. ft.) or large (about 200,000 sq. ft.). Small warehouses could handle a flow of up to 2 million units per year whereas large warehouses could handle a flow of up to 4 million units per year. The current warehouse in St. Louis was small. The fixed and variable costs of small and large warehouses in different locations are shown in Table 6-2.

Table 6-1　Demand for each customer zone in 1999

Zone	Demand in 1999	Zone	Demand in 1999
Northwest	320,000	Lower Midwest	220,000
Southwest	200,000	Northeast	350,000
Upper Midwest	260,000	Southeast	175,000

Table 6-2　The fixed and variable costs of small and large warehouses

Location	Small Warehouse		Large Warehouse	
	Fixed cost /($/year)	Variable cost /($/unit flow)	Fixed cost /($/year)	Variable cost /($/unit flow)
Seattle	300,000	0.20	500,000	0.20
Denver	250,000	0.20	420,000	0.20
St. Louis	220,000	0.20	375,000	0.20
Atlanta	220,000	0.20	375,000	0.20
Philadelphia	240,000	0.20	400,000	0.20

Sanjay estimated that the **inventory holding costs**[3] at a warehouse (excluding warehouse expense) was about $600 *$F$, where F is the number of units flowing through the warehouse per year. Thus, a warehouse handling 1,000,000 units per year incurred an inventory holding cost of $600,000 in the course of the year. Inventory cost calculating formulas are shown in Table 6-3.

Table 6-3 Inventory Cost calculating formulas

Range of F	Inventory Cost
0-2 million	$250,000 + 0.310F
2-4 million	$530,000 + 0.170F
4-6 million	$678,000 + 0.133F
Over 6 million	$798,000 + 0.113F

SportStuff charged a flat fee of $3 per shipment sent to a customer. An average customer order contained four units. SportStuff in turn contracted with UPS to handle all its **outbound shipments**[4]. UPS charges were based on both the origin and the destination of the shipment and are shown in Table 6-4. Management estimated that inbound transportation costs for shipments from suppliers were likely to remain unchanged, no matter what the warehouse configuration selected.

Table 6-4 UPS charges

	Northwest	Southwest	Upper Midwest	Lower Midwest	Northeast	Southeast
Seattle	$2.00	$2.50	$3.50	$4.00	$5.00	$5.50
Denver	$2.50	$2.50	$2.50	$3.00	$4.00	$4.50
St. Louis	$3.50	$3.50	$2.50	$2.50	$3.00	$3.50
Atlanta	$4.00	$4.00	$3.00	$2.50	$3.00	$2.50
Philadelphia	$4.50	$5.00	$3.00	$3.50	$2.50	$4.00

New specialized terms

1. venture capitalist　风险资本家
2. level off　维持平稳
3. inventory holding cost　存货持有成本
4. outbound shipment　外埠运输

Case summary

SportStuff 公司的增长计划

2000年12月，Sanjay Gupta 正在与他的管理团队忙着评估上年的业绩。今年的需求增长了80%。然而，这种增长是喜忧参半。支持该公司的风险资本家对销售的增长和由此带来的收入增长感到非常高兴。然而，Sanjay 和他的团队清楚地认识到，如果需求持续增长，而供应链网络不重新设计，成本的增长将快于收入的增长。于是，他们决定分析公司目前的网络绩效，探寻重新设计供应链网络的模式，以最好地适应下一个三年快速增长的需求。

Sanjay Gupta 在 1996 年创立了 Sportstuff 公司，其使命是向一些家长提供买得起的子女所需的运动设备。父母们抱怨不得不扔掉昂贵的溜冰鞋、滑雪板、夹克和鞋子，因为孩子们长得太快，穿不下它们了。最初的计划是收购已用过的运动装备和衣服或者生产者或零售商多余的产品通过网上营销，这一想法取得了良好的业绩——1996 年底获得了 80 万美元的销售额，并得到了很多风险资本的支持。

1996 年 6 月，公司租了圣·路易斯郊外的一个仓库，供应商将产品运送到此地，客户的订单在此打包并由 UPS 运输。随着需求的增长，Sportstuff 在仓库租用了更多的空间。到 1999 年公司已租下全部仓库，产品运到美国各地的客户。管理层将全美划分为 6 个顾客群，1999 年每个地区的需求总额如表 6-1 所示。Sanjay 预见未来三年公司需求将会每年增长 80%，然后稳定下来，因此需要更多的仓库来应付预期的增长。一个可选方案是在圣·路易斯租用更多的仓库；其他的方案是，在全美范围内租用仓库。租用仓库涉及固定成本（根据仓库的大小计算）和可变成本（根据运送产品的数量而定）。公司在西雅图、丹佛、亚特兰大和费城确定了 4 个潜在的仓库位置。不同地点的大、小仓库费用如表 6-2 所示。租用的仓库中小的面积为 10 万平方英尺，大的面积为 20 万平方英尺；小仓库每年货流量为 200 万件，大的为 400 万件，目前在圣·路易斯租用的是小仓库。

Sanjay 估计了一下存货成本（不含仓库费）大约为 $600*F$，F 代表每年的货流量。那么，一年中一个仓库处理 100 万件产品大约需要存货成本 60 万美元。存货成本核算公式见表 6-3。SportStuff 公司为一件产品支付大约 3 美元运输费，一个客户订单包含 4 件产品。SportStuff 公司将其所有外埠运输业务交付给 UPS 运作，UPS 根据原产地和目的地收费（如表 6-4）。管理层估计不管如何配置仓库，来自供应商的内向运输成本保持不变。

▶ Questions for discussion

1. What is the cost SportStuff incurs if all warehouses leased are in St. Louis?
2. What supply chain network configuration do you recommend for SportStuff?

▶ Hint for analysis and Reference answer

1. What is the cost SportStuff incurs if all warehouses leased are in St. Louis?

The warehousing cost is the function of inventory holding cost, warehouse leasing cost and transportation cost. In 1999, the total cost SportStuff incurs if all warehouses leased are in St. Louis is $2,418,375 (525+722.75+1,170.625).

2. What supply chain network configuration do you recommend for SportStuff?

In 2000, the total demand reached 27,450,000 (57,600, 360,000, 468,000, 396,000, 630,000, 315,000), the total cost SportStuff incurs if all warehouses leased are in St. Louis is $4,022,125 (905,000+1,010,000+2,107,125). When total demand reached 4,941,000, leasing large warehouses in Denver and Atlanta is more cost-effective compared with leasing only in St. Louis. When total demand reached 8,893,800, adding warehouses in Philadelphia and Seattle is more reasonable. You need to determine the location and the size of and the number of units flowing through the warehouse per year. Based upon the above information, you can configure a specific supply chain network.

Case 18

Birth of a Sweater

How does today's global supply chain work? Take the seemingly simple task of creating a linen sweater by Eileen Fisher, a Li & Fung customer. Eileen Fisher supplies the design, boxes of labels and the address of a warehouse in Irvington, New York. Li & Fung chooses and hires all the suppliers and sub-suppliers and arranges shipments from the raw materials stage to the warehouse. "We stitch together supply chains," says managing director William Fung, four years younger than Victor.

Here's one of them: Every two months a 150-ton shipment of high-quality flax leaves France for the 40-day boat ride to Tianjin, a port on the eastern coast of China. The **bales**[1] are loaded onto trucks for the 255-mile drive west to Shuozhou, a traditional coal-mining city of 1.3 million people that's about 200 miles from Beijing. On downtown streets donkeys pull wooden carts piled high with leeks until they (the donkeys, not the leeks) are stir-fried in a favorite local dish.

Inside the gates of Shanxi Shuofang Flax Textile, a state-owned company, a dozen peasant women wearing face masks sit in a warehouse amid mountains of French flax. They pick straw and other impurities out of what looks and smells like hay in a barn. The cleaned flax is taken to the building next door, where it is fed into a series of French-made machines that spin and comb it into long strands that look like a teenager's blond ponytail. The machines were shipped to Shanxi Shuofang a decade ago after a French factory closed when it became cheaper to spin yarn in China. This is the only factory in China with such sophisticated equipment, according to the factory manager. The combed flax, soft as hair, is bleached, dried and fed into another set of machines that spin the fiber into yarn and roll it onto spools. Working around the clock in three shifts, the factory's 750 workers spin the flax into 2,000 spools of yarn a day to earn their $1.25-to-$2 daily wage. Five women sit on the floor and pack each 10-inch **spool**[2] into plastic bags, which are put on trucks and driven 1,116 miles south to Guangzhou. In a factory there the yarn is dyed lime green, pink, white, coral or purple.

Fourteen hours after dyeing begins, the colorful yarn is put on another truck for the two-hour drive to Everbright Knitting Factory in Dongguan, not far from Hong Kong. There's a basketball court in the factory courtyard there for future Yao Mings, workers' dormitories have a **complimentary**[3] cell phone charging station, and unskilled workers earn $4 a day—nearly twice the region's minimum wage—all in an effort to hold on to employees in southern China's export hothouse.

Colorful spools of yarn are taken from the **loading dock**[4] to the factory's third floor, where workers stand ready at 400 knitting machines. The yarn is woven into linen panels, which are linked together with special sewing machines until a sweater takes shape. Each is pulled over a torso-shaped fluorescent light and checked. Ninety-five percent pass inspection and are thrown into 4-foot-tall washing machines, then into giant dryers. When they come out, the rough linen feels soft. They are ironed, Eileen Fisher labels are hand-stitched to the sweaters, there's another quality check, and finally **price tags**[5] with **bar codes**[6] are attached. The price is $148—more than a month's wages for the workers who stitched the sweaters together and four months' wages for those in the flax-combing factory. The goods are packed by hand into dear bags, then placed into **cardboard boxes**[7].

Those boxes are sent down the **freight elevator**[8] and put on trucks for the two-hour drive across the Chinese border to a Hong Kong shipper's warehouse. Ninety percent of *Li & Fung's* clothing shipments go by boat, but more expensive clothing or brands that aim at the most fickle fashion set are shipped by **air freight**[9]. At the Trans Global Logistics warehouse in Hong Kong the sweater boxes are counted, weighed, measured and slapped with a **bar-coded sticker**[10] that contains shipping details. Then it's into 5-foot-high metal airport cargo containers and onto yet another truck for the half-hour drive to the Hong Kong-airport's cargo loading facility. Seven minutes after the truck drives through the airport's guarded gate, the Eileen Fisher goods glide down a giant **conveyor belt**[11] to an oversize X-ray machine. One recent shipment headed for John F. Kennedy Airport via Seoul on Asiana Airlines, the Korean carrier with the lowest air freight rate that week for 800 pounds of brightly colored sweaters.

One boat, three factories, five trucks and two airplanes later, the French flax had journeyed nearly around the world, reincarnated as a designer sweater ready for Christmas shoppers in Manhattan's stylish Soho neighborhood.

In the mid-1990s *Li & Fung* acquired the Eileen Fisher account when it bought a company called Dodwell and set about deepening the relationship. Dodwell simply found a factory to produce what the firm told it to. The *Fung* brothers went deeper, including offering sources for yarn and other materials. "She does very nice, elegant styles, and the fabrics are key," William says. If styles change and Eileen Fisher needs fabrics with crinkles, *Li & Fung* can source from its Indian suppliers.

Questions for discussion

1. How is Li Fung's apparel supply chain stitched together? Can you map out its supply chain?

2. How does Li Fung create value both for the client and for itself?

New specialized terms

1. bale　捆，包
2. spool　线轴
3. complimentary　免费的
4. loading dock　装货月台
5. price tag　价格标签
6. bar code　条形码
7. cardboard box　纸箱
8. freight elevator　货运电梯
9. air freight　航空运输
10. bar-coded sticker　条码标签
11. conveyor belt　传送带

Case summary

针织衫的诞生——利丰

通过 Eileen Fisher 和利丰的合作展示了现代供应链的运作方式。作为客户，Eileen Fisher 只需要提供设计，标签盒和位于纽约欧文顿的成品仓库的地址，利丰选择和雇用所有的供应商和子供应商，并安排从原材料阶段到仓库的发货。该公司的总经理 William Fung 表示："我们将供应链连接在一起。"William Fung 比 Victor 小 4 岁。

利丰每隔两个月会将原产于法国的 150 吨优质亚麻经由海运运到天津，再把一捆捆亚麻再装上货车运往 255 英里外的朔州。朔州是一个传统的煤矿城市，人口 130 万，距离北京约 200 英里。在市中心的街道上，驴子拉着高高的装满韭菜的木车，直到它们（是驴子，不是韭菜）被炒成当地最受欢迎的菜肴。

在一个国营纺织厂内，十几个农妇戴着口罩把杂质去除。然后亚麻被投入隔壁的世界上最先进的法国的纺织机，把亚麻梳理成长条。十年前法国工厂关闭的时候，这些纺织机就运来了。据工厂管理人员介绍，这是中国唯一拥有如此先进设备的工厂。梳理过的亚麻被漂白烘干投入纺织机，纺成亚麻线，然后卷到线轴上。工人们三班倒，750 个工人一天能纺 2 000 个线轴，每天的工资从 1.25 美元到 2 美元不等。5 位女工坐在地上把线轴装入塑料袋，装上卡车后运往 1 116 公里外的广州。在广州的工厂里，亚麻纱线被染成石灰绿，粉红色，白色，珊瑚色或者紫色。

染色 14 小时后，彩色纱线被装入另一辆卡车，经过 2 小时的运输送到东莞的永明针织厂。在那里工厂为了留人，在厂区内为未来的"姚明"们设了篮球场，工人的宿舍安装了免费的手机充电站，非熟练工一天都能挣4美元，是当地最低工资标准的2倍。

彩色线轴被从装货月台运到工厂三层，工人们在400台纺织机前，把纱线纺成亚麻布块，再用特制的缝纫机把布块缝成衣服。每件衣服都要经过检查，95%的衣服通过了检查，被投进4英尺高的洗衣机，然后是巨大的烘干机。从机器出来后，粗糙的亚麻变的很软，经过熨烫，手工缝上Eileen Fisher标签，再经过一次质检，最终贴上带条码的价格标签。售价是148美元，比中国亚麻梳理厂工人4个月工资还高。衣服被手工包装进昂贵的袋子，再装入纸箱。

装了箱的亚麻衣服下货运电梯后又被装上卡车，经过两小时运输送到香港的发货人仓库。利丰90%的衣服采用海运，但是昂贵的衣服或时装品牌选择空运。在全球物流公司的香港仓库，箱子经过清点、称重、测量、贴物流标签，被装入5英尺高的金属制航空集装箱，再经过半小时的公路运输送到香港机场的货场。进了机场大门7分钟后，Eileen Fisher的货物从巨大的传送带滑向特大的X光机，将搭乘最近一班韩亚航空经由首尔前往肯尼迪机场的航班出运，该承运人本周为800磅以上的彩色服装提供最优惠的运费。

法国亚麻经过一次海运，三家工厂，五次汽运，两次空运，周游了整个地球，重生为一件圣诞季在曼哈顿高档街区销售的时装。

利丰集团在20世纪90年代中期买下名叫Dodwell的公司时接管了Eileen Fisher的账户，并开始深化双方的关系。Dodwell只是简单地找了一家工厂，按照公司的要求进行生产。冯氏兄弟更进一步，包括提供纱线和其他材料的来源。"她做得很棒，很优雅，面料是关键。"William说。如果Eileen Fisher的设计风格转变，需要带褶皱的布料，利丰则会从印度采购。

▶ Hint for analysis and Reference answer

1. How is Li Fung's apparel supply chain stitched together? Can you map out its supply chain?

In the apparel supply chain, Li Fung acts as the core enterprise. In the downstream, there are clients that outsource their production and distribution to Li Fung. In the upstream, there are many raw materials suppliers, production factories around the world ready for cooperation with Li Fung, and many logistics service providers offer their service to Li Fung.

The network chain structure should be mapped with Li Fung as the core, with upper stream suppliers and down stream clients.

2. How does Li Fung create value both for the client and for itself?

Li Fung is the first company to propose "soft three dollars" idea, that is, to reduce logistics cost by optimizing the logistics network. By owning almost every process of production and distribution, and making use of its worldwide resources, Li Fung helps the client to concentrate on processes that the client is good at, like branding and marketing. Meanwhile, Li Fung improves its importance as a global supply chain management company, as well as creates profits.

Case 19

Dell Computers: using the supply chain to compete

The personal computer sector was still in its infancy when, in 1983, medical student Michael Dell began buying up remainder stocks of outdated IBM PCs from local retailers, upgrading them in his college dorm, and then selling them on at bargain prices to eager consumers. Dell abandoned his studies soon afterwards to concentrate on his growing computer business. By 1985 his company, Dell Computers, had switched from upgrading old IBMs to building its own machines, but Dell was different from other computer manufacturers of its day. The machines themselves were technologically unremarkable, but it was the way in which they were sold-directly to the customer—that gave Dell a unique advantage over established, product-focused, PC makers.

While the industry leaders vied amongst themselves to introduce PCs with ever more impressive technology, little consideration was given to the mundane business of supply chain management. The computers they produced were invariably **made-to-forecast**[1] and because of the way they were sold—through shops, resellers, and systems integrators—were then destined to languish for an average of two months in warehouses or on shop shelves before being purchased by the customer. Meanwhile Dell remained focused on the end user, thus avoiding the inherent double jeopardy created by the dynamics and economics of the industry. Firstly, around 80 percent of the costs of manufacturing a PC are component costs, and component costs have been falling since the industry's inception, particularly the all-important processors that continue to fall in price by an average of 30 percent per year. The longer these components wait to be sole, the worse value they become. Secondly, there is the risk that a step-change in technology may make millions of pounds' worth of finished PCs obsolete overnight, forcing manufacturers to either compensate resellers for unloading stocks at a loss, or incur the costs of shipping them to developing countries where they can be sold off cheaply.

By selling directly to the customer, Dell was able to configure and assemble every PC to order, thus avoiding the risks associated with carrying finished inventory, which in turn enabled it to maintain its cost advantage over its conventional rivals. Dell's low-priced machines with their bespoke configuration became an attractive alternative for those customers who were confident enough to buy direct.

For many years, received wisdom in the industry considered Dell's position to be nothing more than that of a successful **niche player**[2]. It was widely believed that the majority of business-to-business customers and indeed consumers buying PCs for the home, would always prefer to purchase their equipment through traditional channels, where help would be at hand should something go wrong and consumers could see and touch the products before purchase. In a bid to break out of its perceived niche, Dell embarked on a brief flirtation with conventional retail distribution channels. The move was a mistake. Retail sales plummeted as soon as Dell offered a new PC through its direct channels. Dell was obliged to compensate the retailers for their losses. As a result, the company posted its first ever loss ($36m) in 1993. The ill-judged foray was a salutary lesson in the perils of attempting to operate through conflicting distribution channels and a vindication of its original low-cost **direct sales strategy**[3].

Dell pulled out of the retail market in 1994 and retrenched with a vengeance, rebounding immediately with profits of $149m. From this point on Dell concentrated on finding ways to leverage the strengths of its original direct sales strategy, concentrating on minimizing inventory and increasing return on capital employed. Leanness, flexibility and above all time compression were the keys. Over the next three years Dell's operations were closely reexamined to squeeze every possible moment of **non-value adding time**[4] out of its procurement and assembly processes. By 1997, Dell was not only a model of JIT manufacturing, but had applied its own exacting time standards to the rest of its supply chain. It had specified that the majority of components have to be warehoused within 15 minutes of Dell's three factories (in Austin, Texas; Limerick, Ireland; Penang, Malaysia), and many components are not ordered from a supplier before Dell receives a customer order. To achieve such levels of co-operation and integration, Dell has reduced its number of suppliers from 204 companies in 1992 to just 47. At the same time, it has preferred to source from suppliers close to their plants rather than from more distant offshore suppliers, even though the local manufacturing costs may be higher.

For Dell's Limerick plant, at least 40 percent of components are produced and supplied on a JIT basis, a further 45 percent of components are held in supplier hubs, located close to Dell's factory, the suppliers restock their own warehouses and manage their own inventories, delivering to the factories on a consignment stock basis. Bulky finished subassemblies, such as monitors and speakers are treated differently. Instead of shipping them to Dell's factories, they are sent directly to the customer from the suppliers' hub (located close to the market rather than close to Dell's factory), saving Dell approximately $30 per item in freight costs. Dell is billed for the components only when they leave the suppliers' warehouse in response to a customer order, so that the components themselves are likely to spend only half a day as Dell's own inventory. The supplier receives payment approximately 45 days later.

Where the suppliers of essential components (such as disk drives) cannot be assembled as quickly as the computers can be bolted together, Dell is pressing the suppliers to shorten their own lead times, but in the meantime, their components must be built to forecast. Fortunately, demand for components is much more predictable than demand for finished goods, though shortages of some critical components (most noticeably microprocessors) continue to be a problem across the industry. Here again, the direct sales method places Dell at an advantage over those makers who use traditional routes to market. Because Dell communicates directly with its customers, it is able to shape demand through its telephone sales by steering customers towards configurations using readily available components.

Meanwhile Dell has forged ahead with Internet sales as an even more cost-effective version of its direct-sales approach. Dell is not the first or the only PC retailer to venture into cyberspace, though by 1997 it was certainly the most successful, mainly because no other manufacturer was better placed to make such a move. Within six months of opening for business through its Website, Dell was clocking up Internet sales of $1m per day, with sales through the channel growing by 20 percent per month. Far from remaining a small niche option, direct buyers now account for a third of all PC sales in the US, up from only 15 percent in 1991. Internet sales have been slower to take-off in Europe and Asia, but they are rising and are set to climb higher in these increasingly computer literate societies.

To place an order, customers simply dial into the Website and follow the on-screen instructions. The software allows them to monitor on-screen the price impact of each option as they configure their PC, then tap in their credit card or account payment details, before finally placing the order at the click of a mouse. The customer receives confirmation of the order within five minutes of its placement, not more than 36 hours later their bespoke PCs are trundling off the production lines and onto the delivery trucks. Most of this time is spent not assembling the machines, but testing the machines and loading software. Dell can expect to see payment for most sales within 24 hours of order placement, while rivals such as PC market leader, Compaq, must wait around 35 days for payment through primary dealers. Even other direct sellers are apt to take over a fortnight to convert an order in cash.

By the end of 1997, Dell was growing at a rate that was more than three times the industry average and had become the world's second biggest PC maker (by unit sales). Third quarter revenues were up 58 percent to $3,188 m. Finished goods inventory and **work in progress**[5] stood at a combined figure of just $57 m, with a further $244 m in raw material and other items, giving a total inventory of around 11 days of sales. Dell's growth and return on investment are the envy of the industry and have been reflected in the staggering rise of Dell's stock price. Other established industry players have tried to emulate Dell's direct sales formula, but have retreated after running into the same channel conflicts as Dell had encountered in 1993 with it's foray into retail sales. In the meantime, Dell is moving on to its next big growth opportunity the network server business where through its partnership with network equipment manufacturer 3Com Corp, it hopes to apply its PC and time-saving know-how to reduce the lengthy period needed to test the compatibility of each newly launched computer or networking device. By supplying 3Com with new computers as soon as they are introduced, the partners hope to slash the existing 60-90 days testing period for new equipment to just two weeks. Acting together to bring new solutions to the market more quickly, the partners were set to outpace their rivals and make a lasting impression on the network server business.

Questions for discussion

1. What is Dell's supply chain strategy? How Dell operate its logistics network?
2. How much benefit did Dell gain from its supply chain operation? Briefly describe the performance of Dell's supply chain, for example in inventory, lead time.
3. In your opinion, what can Chinese companies learn from Dell's success in logistics and supply chain operation?

New specialized terms

1. made-to-forecast 按预测生产
2. niche player 市场钻缝者
3. direct sales strategy 直销策略
4. non-value adding time 非增值活动占用的时间
5. work in progress 在制品

Case summary

Dell：利用供应链开展竞争

在个人电脑（PC）仍处于起步期的 1983 年，医疗专业的学生 Dell 低价买入 IBM 公司过时的模块，并在自己的大学宿舍里进行升级，然后以低廉的价格出售给渴望购买这些电脑的消费者。随后他放弃学业专注于电脑业务并在 1985 年成立了自己的公司，销售 Dell 计算机，但 Dell 与当时的其他电脑制造商不同。机器技术上不出色，但是却运用了直销方式，这形成了 Dell 独一无二的竞争优势。

当行业领先者致力于 PC 技术差异化竞争时，他们很少考虑平淡无奇的供应链管理业务。他们根据预测制造的计算机，因为通过商店、中间商和系统集成商销售，到达顾客手中之前在仓库或货架上平均滞留两个月。与此同时，Dell 致力于终端客户，从而规避了行业的双重风险。首先，由于 PC 发展初期，产品 80%的成本来自组装，然而处理器的价格每年平均以 30%的速度下降。这些组件等待使用的时间越长，它们的价值越低。其次，技术更新换代导致库存 PC 一夜之间过时，损失严重，迫使制造商要么赔偿经销商的损失，要么承担低价售给发展中国家的运输成本。

通过直销的方式，Dell 能根据订单组装 PC，避免了持有成品库存的风险，从而树立了相对于传统竞争者的成本优势。Dell 的可定制配置的低价机器对自信直接购买的客户很有吸引力。

多年来，行业对 Dell 的定位只不过是成功的市场钻缝者。他们深信大多数顾客，还是习惯于从可感知的传统渠道购买，因为电脑一旦出现问题，总能得到帮助。于是 Dell 也开始冲破市场缝隙，尝试传统零售渠道。这种转型决策是错误的。只要直销新电脑，零售额就急剧下降，Dell 不得不赔偿零售商由此带来的损失。1993 年首次出现的 3 600 万美元的赔偿给 Dell 带来了教训，双重销售模式的冲突证实了低成本直销战略的可行性。

Dell 在 1994 年撤离传统渠道，其利润迅速反弹，达到 1.49 亿美元。从此 Dell 专注于发挥直销战略的优势、最小化存货、增加资本回报。精益化、灵活性以及最重要的缩短时间才是关键。接下来的三年 Dell 在采购和组装环节反复压缩非增值活动占用的时间。到了 1997 年，Dell 不仅仅是准时制的制造商，而且还向其余供应链成员提出了精准的时间标准。Dell 具体要求零部件 15 分钟以内到位，并且在接到顾客订单之前许多部件并不从供应商那里订购，为此大大减少了供应商数量，从 1992 年的 204 家减少到 47 家。与此同时，Dell 优先考虑选择距离工厂近的供应商，尽管当地制造的成本会高一些。

工厂至少 40%的零部件在准时制基础上生产和供应，另有 45%的部件会存放在靠近 Dell 工厂的当地供应商的物流中心。供应商给自己的仓库进货并管理自己的库存，再以寄售方式配送到工厂。区别对待显示器和扬声器之类的笨重成品部件，部分组件不送到 Dell 工厂而是直接从供应商那里送到顾客那里，靠近市场而不是靠近 Dell 的工厂，每件产品大约为 Dell 节约了 30 美元的运费，这样能节约时间和费用，加快资金周转。只有当这些组件响应客户订单离开仓库时，Dell 才会为这些组件付费，因此这些组件本身作为 Dell 的库存可能只需要半天时间。供应商大约在 45 天后收到货款。

当供应商的主要部件（如磁盘驱动器）不能被迅速组合时，Dell 就会给供应商施加压力以缩短他们的供应时间，但与此同时，他们的部件必须根据预测生产。由于部件相对于成品其需求更易预测，尽管某些关键部件（最明显的是微处理器）的短缺仍然是整个行业的一个问题。Dell 在这方面再次体现出相比传统渠道的优势。因为可以与客户实现直接沟通，Dell 可以通过电话销售状况引导客户的需求，使其使用当前可用的配件。

Dell 打造了自己在网路销售方面的优势。虽然不是最先和唯一进入网络销售的商家，但是取得了最大的成就，主要是因为没有其他制造商更好地做出这样的举动。在 6 个月内通过其开放网站，1997 年每天的网上销售额高达 100 万美元，而且每月以 20%的速度增长。远不是在市场分一杯羹而已，在美国，直销额占了电脑总销售额的三分之一，而 1991 年互联网销售额仅占 15%。网络销售在欧亚地区起步较慢，但在这类"机民"率日益提高的社会将不断攀升。

要下单,客户只需登录网站,按照屏幕上的指示操作。在 Dell 的网络销售系统中,顾客可以完成选择电脑配置并监控不同选项对价格的影响,然后点击信用卡或账户支付信息,最后点击鼠标下单完成电子支付,顾客订单会在 5 分钟内获得确认,36 小时内他们定制的电脑就会从生产线上下来,装上送货卡车。大部分时间不是花在装配机器上,而是花在测试和加载软件上。Dell 公司在 24 小时内收到订单支付款,远远优于竞争对手如 PC 市场领导者——Compaq 的 35 天。其他直销商则需要两周时间才能把订单变为现金。

截至 1997 年底,Dell 以高于行业 3 倍的增长率,成为世界第二大 PC 制造商(按单位销售额计算)。第三季度收入增长 58%,达到 3.18 亿美元。成品库存和在制品总额仅为 5 700 万美元,原材料和其他物资的库存只有 2.44 亿美元,销售总库存时间只有 11 天。Dell 的投资回报率与股价均令业界垂涎。其他老牌同行试图模仿 Dell 的模式,但是又因陷入与 Dell 1993 年经历的涉足门店销售相同的渠道冲突而撤出。Dell 开始通过与网络设备制造商 3Com 公司的合作进军下一个具备高增长潜力的网络服务器行业。Dell 希望应用其 PC 和省时的诀窍减少新推出的电脑网络设备的兼容测试时间。双方希望通过合作将新设备测试期从 60～90 天缩短到 2 周,以便超越对手向市场更快推出新的解决方案,在网络服务器行业获取持久竞争力。

Hint for analysis and Reference answer

1. What is Dell's supply chain strategy? How does Dell operate its logistics network?

Over 40 percent of Dell's components are produced and supplied on a JIT basis, a further 45 percent of components are held in supplier hubs, located close to Dell's factory. The suppliers restock their own warehouses and manage their own inventories, delivering to the factories on a consignment stock basis, such as monitors and speakers are treated differently. Instead of shipping bulky finished subassemblies to Dell's factories, they are sent directly to the customer from the suppliers' logistics center (located close to the market), saving Dell much time and freight costs.

2. How much benefit did Dell gain from its supply chain operation? Briefly describe the performance of Dell's supply chain, for example in inventory, lead time.

Dell has forged ahead with Internet sales as an even more cost-effective version of its direct-sales approach. Within six months of opening for business through its Website, Dell was clocking up Internet sales of $1m per day, with sales through the channel growing by 20 percent per month.

By 1997, Dell was not only a model of JIT manufacturing, but had applied its own exacting time standards to the rest of its supply chain. It had specified that the majority of components have to be warehoused within 15 minutes of Dell's three factories, and many components are not ordered from a supplier before Dell receives a customer order. To achieve such levels of co-operation and integration, Dell has reduced its number of suppliers from 204 companies in 1992 to just 47. At the same time, it has preferred to source from suppliers close to their plants rather than from more distant oversea suppliers.

3. In your opinion, what can Chinese companies learn from Dell's success in logistics and supply chain operation?

Chinese companies should focus on minimizing inventory, increasing return on capital, improving the flexibility of their supply chain through cooperating with their upstream and downstream partners and effective information sharing with end users, implementing JIT manufacturing and trying to squeeze every possible moment of non-value adding time out of their procurement and assembly processes.

Part Seven

International Logistics

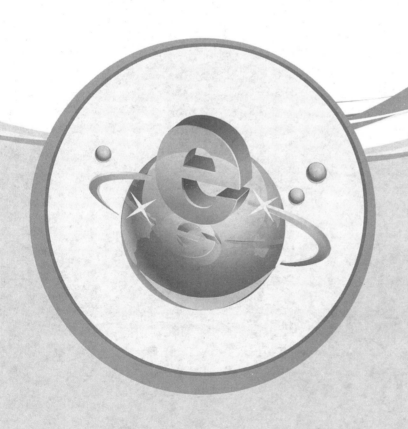

Part Seven　International Logistics

After learning this part, you will be able to:
● Gain an understanding of the characteristics of international logistics
● Identify strategic options in international logistics
● Discuss factors impacting a firm's entering overseas markets
● Discuss the types of international logistics intermediaries

Case 20

Where to produce?

　　Barbara Linse is a procurement manager of shirts for a chain of men' wear stores in Chicago. Currently they are selling clothing made in the United States. In its Houston, Texas plant, a dress shirt can be produced for $8 per shirt (including the cost of raw materials). Chicago is a major market for 100,000 shirts per year. **Transportation and storage**[1] charges from Houston to Chicago amount to $5 per **hundredweight (cwt.)**[2]. Each packaged shirt weighs 1 pound.

　　Since Asia has gained importance as world production center, Barbara Linse is thinking about changing the production site of the dress shirt. After contacting with her Asian partner, Barbara Linse finds out that the company can have the shirts produced in Taiwan for $4 per shirt (including the cost of raw materials). The raw materials, weighing about 1 pound per shirt, would be shipped from Houston to Taiwan at a cost of $2 per cwt. When the shirts are completed, they are to be shipped directly to Chicago at a transportation and storage cost of $6 per cwt. An **import duty**[3] of $0.50 per shirt is assessed.

▷ Questions for discussion

1. From production and logistics cost perspective, should the company produce the dress shirts in Houston or in Taiwan?
2. What are the other factors, other than cost, should be taken into consideration before the final decision is made?

New specialized terms

1. transportation and storage　运输和仓储
2. hundredweight (cwt.)　英担（一百磅）
3. import duty　进口税

Case summary

在哪生产？

Barbara Linse 是芝加哥男装连锁店的男士衬衫采购经理。目前他们主要销售美国生产的衣服。在位于得克萨斯州休斯敦市的工厂，一件时髦衬衫的生产成本是8美元（包括原材料成本）。芝加哥每年需要10万件衬衫进行销售。从休斯敦到芝加哥的运输和存储成本为每英担（百磅）5美元。每件包装的重量约为1磅。

自从亚洲日益成为世界生产中心，Barbara Linse 考虑改变其生产场所。经过和她的亚洲商业伙伴联系，Barbara Linse 得知该公司可以在台湾以每件4美元（包括原材料成本）的成本生产。每件衬衫的原材料重约1磅，需要以每英担（百磅）2美元的价格由休斯敦运到台湾。衬衫生产出来后，需要从台湾直接运到芝加哥，每英担（百磅）的运输和仓储成本为6美元。报关时每件衬衫需要支付0.5美元的进口税。

Hint for analysis and Reference answer

1. From production and logistics cost perspective, should the company produce the dress shirts in Houston or in Taiwan?

This problem introduces the student to the evaluation of alternate channels of production and distribution. To know whether domestic or foreign production is least expensive, the total cost of production and distribution must be computed from the source point to the marketplace.

Two alternatives are suggested and they can be compared as follows.

Production at Houston:

　　Total cost = Production cost at Houston + Transportation and storage costs

　　　　= \$8/shirt × 100,000 shirts + \$5/cwt. × 1,000 cwt.

　　　　= \$805,000/year

Production at Taiwan:

Total cost = Production cost in Taiwan + Transportation and storage costs from Taiwan to Chicago

　　　+ Import duty + Raw material transportation cost from Houston to Taiwan

　　　= \$4/shirt × 100,000 shirts + \$6/cwt. × 1,000 cwt. + \$0.5/shirt × 100,000 shirts + \$2/cwt. × 1,000 cwt.

= $458,000/year

Producing in Taiwan would appear to be the least expensive.

2. What are the other factors, other than cost, should be taken into consideration before the final decision is made?

Other factors to consider before a final decision is made might be:

(1) How reliable would international transportation be compared with domestic transportation?

(2) What is the business climate in Taiwan such that costs might change in favor of Houston as a production point?

(3) How likely is it that the needed transportation and storage will be available?

(4) If the market were to expand, would there be adequate production capacity available to support the increased demand?

Case 21

Betty's Brownies

Growing up in Chicago, Betty Budris always enjoyed baking: cookies, cakes, sweets of all kinds. As Betty's children grew up, all their friends knew that Betty was the neighborhood source for **homemade treats**[1]. But once Betty's children had gone off to college, she was left with lots of time-tested **recipes**[2] but few "consumers." Her son Kenny was working on his MBA in marketing at Northwestern University when he suggested to his mom that they go into business together and bring Betty's treats to the sweet teeth of the world.

They started small, with a **walk-in bakery shop**[3] in Evanston, Illinois, not far from the Northwestern campus. Wildly successful with the college crowd, they expanded by building a baking plant in Gurnee, Illinois, where they could concentrate on making packaged cookies and brownies with modifications to Betty's old recipes.

One of Betty's first corporate customers was ABC Sky Kitchen, an airport-based caterer who specialized in assembling meals for in-flight food service. One of their customers was Japan Airlines, and soon Betty's Double Fudge Brownies were being served warm to business-class and first-class passengers on JAL. It wasn't long after ABC Sky Kitchen began to serve the tasty brownies that Kenny received an email message from Ryuji Fujikami in Tokyo. Mr. Fujikami had enjoyed a Betty's Brownie on his return flight to Tokyo, and was interested in the possibility that Betty's might want to export their brownies to Japan. Mr. Fujikami was a food buyer for a major Japanese department store chain, and thus presented an immediate overseas expansion opportunity to Betty's Brownies.

Kenny was excited at the prospects for the company's first step into a distant market. He called Mr. Fujikami to discuss developing a business relationship, and Fujikami responded with an offer to purchase an initial order of 40,000 individually wrapped Double Fudge Brownies. Each packaged brownie would weigh 100 grams (about 3.5 ounces). He asked that the products be labelled in both English and Japanese (for the promotional appeal of the American product), but that Japanese manufacturing standards for food would have to be used to ensure that the brownies would pass customs and agricultural inspection.

The initial order of 40,000 brownies would be shipped to the **department store chain's**[4] distribution center near Osaka, Japan. But Fujikami asked that future shipments be presorted and packaged for direct delivery to the individual retail store locations throughout Japan. Kenny immediately grasped the complexity of this new customer's requirements, and sat down with Betty to consider what kinds of assistance they would need to expand their business into the Japanese market.

Questions for discussion

1. With just one customer in Japan, should Kenny and Betty be handling all aspects of this relationship? What logistics functions might **make sense to outsource**[5]? Which should they consider keeping in house?
2. What transportation modes should be considered for this product? What kinds of **transportation intermediaries**[6] might be useful?
3. Are there roles for specialized logistics intermediaries? List some functions that might be handled by specialists.
4. Assume that Betty's Brownies are a smash success in the Japanese market, and it makes good sense to prepare the raw brownie dough in the Gurnee, Illinois plant, but to then cold-transport it to Osaka for baking and packaging. Revisit your decision regarding specialized logistics intermediaries. List some functions that might be handled by specialists.

New specialized terms

1. homemade treat   家庭自制甜点
2. recipe   食谱；处方
3. walk-in bakery shop   现烤现卖的烘培店
4. department store chain   百货连锁店
5. make sense to outsource   值得外包
6. transportation intermediary   运输中间商

Case summary

贝蒂的甜点

Betty Budris 在芝加哥长大，她总是喜欢烘焙饼干、蛋糕和各种各样的糖果。当 Betty 的孩子长大后，他们所有的朋友都知道 Betty 是邻居们自制美食的来源。但是，Betty 的孩子们上大学后，她只剩下许多久经考验的食谱，但"消费者"却很少。她的儿子 Kenny 当时正在西北大学攻读市场营销的 MBA 学位，他向母亲建议，两人一起经商，让世界各地的人都能尝到 Betty 的美食。

最初他们在 Kenny 所在的大学附近开了一家小型面包店，受到学生好评，之后打算开一家烘焙工厂，改良以前的秘方生产成袋装甜点。

Betty 的第一家企业顾客是一家专做空中食物服务的公司 ABC Sky Kitchen，而这家公司的其中之一客户是日本航空公司，不久之后，Betty 的双层软糖甜点就出现在日本航空公司的商务舱和头等舱里。不久之后，Betty 接到日本的 Fujikami 先生——日本连锁百货公司的食品采购者——的邮件，获悉 Fujikami 先生很欣赏他在返回东京的飞机上所尝的 Betty 的甜点，对 Betty 是否愿意将产品出口到日本非常感兴趣。

Betty 对于公司的第一次海外扩张感到很兴奋，于是打电话给 Fujikami 探讨业务，Fujikami 开始便订购了 40 000 个单独包装的双层软糖甜点，每包重 100 克，大约 3.5 盎司。为了提高美国产品的吸引力，产品包装需要同时用日文和英文，但是必须使用日本食物制造标准以确保该产品能通过海关和农业检测。

首批订购的 40 000 个甜点需要运送到临近日本大阪的连锁百货商店的配送中心。但是 Fujikami 要求未来订购的产品被预先分拣及包装好直接发货到日本的各大零售场所。Kenny 立即掌握了这个新客户要求的复杂性，开始与 Betty 考虑扩大日本市场业务所需要的援助。

◐ Hint for analysis and Reference answer

1. With just one customer in Japan, should Kenny and Betty be handling all aspects of this relationship? What logistics functions might make sense to outsource? Which should they consider keeping in house?

It's not necessary for Kenny and Betty to handle all the businesses connected with brownies logistics in Japan since there is only one customer there. They can outsource the transportation from America to Japan, custom clearance, distribution to established international logistics firms or Japanese logistics providers while focusing on production logistics and internal physical distribution.

2. What transportation modes should be considered for this product? What kinds of transportation intermediaries might be useful?

Air transport and motor transport are suitable for this product. Motor freight forwarder and air freight forwarder are useful in this case.

3. Are there roles for specialized logistics intermediaries? List some functions that might be handled by specialists.

Specialized logistics intermediaries can play a big role here. They can perform functions like freight forward, ship forward, custom clearance, inspection, processing in circulation, information processing and distribution.

4. Assume that Betty's Brownies are a smash success in the Japanese market, and it makes good sense to prepare the raw brownie dough in the Gurnee, Illinois plant, but to

then cold-transport it to Osaka for baking and packaging. Revisit your decision regarding specialized logistics intermediaries. List some functions that might be handled by specialists.

  Since the market potential is large, Kenny and Betty may establish a food processing center in Japan, the subsequent international goods flow will become less. Sea transport combined with road transport is more appropriate and the ocean carriers or international freight forwarder will play a vital role in the new situation. Within Japan, the demand for inbound transportation, packaging, information processing, final distribution and customer service is enlarged. Those functions might be handled by specialists like Japanese third-party logistics providers or co-founded logistics companies with local supermarkets or food chain stores.

Case 22

The Great Bite Peach Company

An item in today's issue of Maritime Outlook Weekly says:

"The first quarter is historically slow for shippers of cargo between Asia and the United States, but ocean carriers in trans-Pacific trades are betting that volumes will rise soon enough—and strong enough—to allow for a $300 rate increase per container on eastbound freight and a second increase in west-bound rates for **refrigerated products**[1]."

"While importers are relying on the reality of several new entrants to keep tonnage at high levels—a fact that usually mitigates against rate increases—exporters are more realistic that the new increases will hold, coming as they do on the heal of the apparent recovery of Asian economies."

"Carriers, meanwhile maintain that US exporters of perishable meat and produce shipments to Asia are growing at pace with the region's return to normalcy after the late 1990s economic crisis. As they begin to redeploy costly refrigerated containers in the Pacific along with specially trained personnel necessary to operate, maintain, and repair them, carriers are looking to improve **freight rates**[2] on westbound hauls."

"Container lines say they have seen increases in reefer cargo volumes ranging from 5 to 11 percent, depending on commodity. They expect the trend to continue for the next six to twelve months as Asian economies strengthen and consumer demand for fresh and chilled meat, fruits, and vegetables from the Americas increases."

"The major carriers in the trade have raised rates on frozen beef, pork, and poultry, French fries and potatoes, fruits and vegetables, juice concentrates, and other refrigerated cargoes beginning January 1, then again February 1, and continuing throughput the year. The lines are expected to implement increases across the board or on an individual basis with amounts and effective dates varying according to commodity, origin, or destination, **seasonal shipping cycles**[3], service requirement, and other factors."

"Carriers are attempting to recover mounting losses, a large portion of which resulted from the Asian economic crisis several years ago. The **ripple effect**[4] of such a **catastrophe-falling exchange rates**[5], reduced lending, contraction of the consumer markets, stifling of consumer confidence—hit the US export market hard as demand went through the floor."

"Meanwhile, the relatively strong U.S. economy and falling Asian exchange rates has created a 20 percent surge in eastbound traffic with another double-digit predicted for the coming six months. This has created a great deal of demand for containers in Asia but much less so in the United States. Carriers have to get containers back to Asia somehow. They are looking to fill back hauls with very little demand."

"Reefer operators are especially vulnerable because there is very little inbound refrigerated traffic. These lines have been forced to offer discounts eastbound. Rates are down across the board. They have fallen to as little as $2,000 per box and less. That is half the rate that existed twelve months earlier for some of the most expensive equipment in the industry."

"But lines report that recent demand has exceeded supply in certain areas for reefer equipment. This specialized equipment now ranges in price from $25,000 to $35,000 per forty-foot box, plus an equivalent amount in repair and maintenance costs over the container's useful life. There are also costs of energy to power the equipment and personnel costs monitoring temperature. Pacific carriers incur further round trip costs because they often are forced to fill their expensive, but less space efficient equipment at lower rates for non-reefer cargo. Shippers say they are expecting some form of westbound rate increase to hold."

You have just been hired as the westbound logistics manager for the Great Bite Peach Company, headquartered in Michigan. The CEO invites to an early Friday afternoon meeting with senior executives of the company including the chief financial officer, the VP of production, and the VP of Sales and Marketing, Ern Hewill, who is excited about the possibility of opening a vast new market in China. One of your current "A" clients, a major American retailer, is opening a chain of supermarts across China and will buy all the fresh peaches you can produce. Upon further questioning, Hewill forecasts 5,000 to 6,000 container loads a year. The VP of production advises there will be no problem meeting the demand. "That is fantastic" says the CEO.

He will look across the table at you. "It's all up to you now," he says. "I must provide a landed cost to our customer as soon as possible, no later than next Wednesday, or they go elsewhere. You get back to your office, call in your freight forwarder and find us a rate."

It's later in the afternoon now in an office overlooking the Seattle waterfront. The sales VP of Pacific Dreams Containership Company has just received a call from Great Bite Peach Company, who has been a customer from time to time. They said that they have the opportunity to sell a great deal of fresh peaches to a major retailer opening a chain of supermarkets across China and need to negotiate an agreement immediately in order to submit to a proposal to their customer. The sales VP arranges a quick meeting with the CEO, Bob Hannus, and the owner's representative. The owner's rep is delighted. "We need this business. Friday's ship has been going out light every week. We have only been operating at 60 percent of capacity westbound for months."

Hannus isn't as animated. He says: "This is reefer cargo. For us to carry this I may have to go out and buy or lease refrigerated equipment. Do you know what that costs?"

The owner's rep says: "We can use the containers on the eastbound with department store merchandise. There is plenty of that."

Hannus looks at his sales VP and says: "Make a deal we can both live with, and don't come back empty handed."

Questions for discussion

1. You are the westbound logistics manager for the Great Bite Peach Company and are about to attempt negotiating a contract. What are the issues as you see them?
2. (continuation of question one.) What other information do you need?
3. You are the sales VP of Pacific Dreams Containership Company and are about to attempt negotiating a contract. What are the issues as you see them?

New specialized terms

1. refrigerated product   冷藏产品
2. freight rate   运费
3. seasonal shipping cycle   季节性运输周期
4. ripple effect   连锁反应
5. catastrophe-falling exchange rate   灾难性的汇率下降

Case summary

味鲜桃公司

根据《海运观察周刊》的信息,对亚洲和美国之间的货运商来说,第一季度是历史性的缓慢时期。但泛太平洋贸易线上的海运承运人认为贸易量很快会强劲上升,因此东向运输的每只集装箱运费可提高 300 美元,西向运输的冷藏货物也可提高运价。

尽管进口商希望新入市的承运人因运量上升抵消运费上涨的影响,可是出口商已经意识到运费上升势头会持续,因为他们在亚洲经济复苏的过程中感受到了这一点。

与此同时,承运人认为,20 世纪 90 年代后期经济危机之后,美国向亚洲出口的鲜肉、农产品也逐渐恢复到正常水平。由于开始在太平洋地区采用昂贵的冷藏集装箱,雇用受过专业训练的人员运营、维护和维修冷藏箱,承运人计划提高美国到亚洲航向的运费。

集装箱船公司说,冷藏货物数量增长了 5% 到 11%,他们认为,随着亚洲经济的好转和对来自美国的鲜肉、冻肉、水果、蔬菜的需求的增加,这种情况会持续6到12个月。

主要承运商已经开始从1月1日起提高了冷冻牛肉、猪肉、家禽、薯条、土豆、水果、蔬菜、浓缩果汁和其他冷冻货物的运费费率,在2月1日又提了价,并且持续了一年。这些船公司可能会根据货物种类、始发地、目的地、季节性航运周期、服务要求和其他因素进行全部或者部分提价,运费提高的程度和日期各有不同。

承运商希望弥补巨额损失,大部分的损失是由于几年前的亚洲经济危机引起的。这场灾难性的汇率降低,借贷减少,消费者市场的紧缩,消费者信心的丧失打击了美国出口市场,需求降到低谷。

同时,相对强劲的美国经济和亚洲的汇率降低导致亚洲到美国的货物量增长了20%,未来6个月还会有两位数的增长。这会让亚洲对集装箱的需求大量增长,而美国对集装箱的需求却没有那么多。承运人不得不把集装箱从美国运回亚洲,但在此过程中能够揽到的货物却很少。

冷藏箱的运营人很受影响,因为亚洲到美国的冷藏货物很少。这些船公司不得不对亚洲到美国方向的货物提供运价折扣。运费总体偏低,每箱降到只有2 000美元或者更少。这只是12个月前运费的一半。

但是根据航线信息显示,在某些地区,冷藏设备的需求已经超过了供应。冷藏箱成本高,40尺箱的购置成本从25 000美元到35 000美元不等,维护成本与此相当,设备还会带来能源成本,监控温度会带来人员成本。太平洋航线上的承运人还会有回程的成本,因为他们不得不用昂贵、空间较小的设备低价运输非冷藏货物。货主认为美国到亚洲的运费会持续目前的增长态势。

味鲜桃公司总部设在密歇根州,你被该公司聘为西向物流部的经理。首席执行官邀请公司高管参加周五下午的会议,包括首席财务官、生产副总裁、销售和市场副总裁 Em Hewill。Em Hewill 对在中国开辟一个巨大新市场的可能性感到非常兴奋。目前有一个大客户在中国开了连锁店,要在那里销售你公司生产的桃,Hewill 预计一年可卖 5 000 到 6 000 个集装箱的桃,生产副总认为生产上没问题。首席执行官说:"那真是棒极了。"他会隔着桌子看着你,"现在全靠你了,"他说,"我必须尽快向我们的客户提供到岸成本,不要晚于下周三,否则他们会去其他地方。你回到办公室后,打电话给你的货运代理,为我们确定一个费率。"

现在是下午晚些时候,在一间俯瞰西雅图海滨的办公室里,太平洋梦幻集装箱公司的销售副总裁刚接到了味鲜桃公司的电话,这家公司经常成为我们的客户。他们说,他们有机会向一家在中国各地开设连锁超市的大型零售商销售大量的桃子,他们需要立即谈判达成协议,以便向客户提交方案。销售副总裁安排了一次与总裁 Bob Hannus 和业主代表的快速会议。业主代表非常开心:"我们需要这笔生意。几个月来船公司每周五西向航行的船舶满载率都只有六成。"

Hannus 就没有那么乐观了。他说:"这是冷藏货物。为了运载它们我不得不外购或租赁冷藏设备。你知道这需要付出什么代价吗?"

业主代表说："我们可以用向东方向的集装箱装百货公司商品。这类商品足够多。"

Hannus 看着他的销售副总裁说："希望做一笔我们都能接受的生意，不要空手而归。"

▷ Hint for analysis and Reference answer

1. You are the westbound logistics manager for the Great Bite Peach Company and are about to attempt negotiating a contract. What are the issues as you see them?

Besides conventional terms in a contract like delivery time, destination and service, freight rate is another issue which needs to be negotiated.

2. (continuation of question one.) What other information do you need?

The logistics manager needs to know the distribution of demand for peaches in each time section since this kind of information is helpful for freight rate negotiation.

3. You are the sales VP of Pacific Dreams Containership Company and are about to attempt negotiating a contract. What are the issues as you see them?

Besides conventional terms in a logistics contract, I will pay attention to clarify the issue of sharing the cost of purchasing or leasing reefer as well as the cost of empty back haul claimed by carriers.

Part Seven   International Logistics

Case 23

Two Countries Compared: Switzerland and Chad

Logistics development in various nations is quite different. The following scenarios are likely to happen. A specific port is not equipped with sufficient **cold-storage**[1] warehousing space, does not have an **appropriately sized crane**[2], or is experiencing delays in getting the goods from the ports to the remainder of the country; a road is particularly congested, a specific tunnel has recently been closed, or a railroad is experiencing **shortage of appropriate cars**[3].

When it comes to assessing the logistics environment of different countries, one cannot find more of a contrast than Switzerland and Chad. These differences serve to illustrate the role of geography, **infrastructure**[4] and **institutions**[5].

Chad is landlocked in the middle of Africa surrounded by countries that also suffer from poor transportation, it only has 200 miles of all-season road. Their per-capita GDP is $600, one of the poorest in Africa, and thus the world. Ironically, it is rich in minerals such as oil, uranium, gold and diamonds and has 50 million acres of arable land. Yet civil strife has prevented economic development since the 1980s. Development for Chad includes money from the World Bank, the European Union, Germany, **the OPEC fund**[6] and France. There are plans for a 700-miles oil pipeline to tap the estimated 900 million barrels of oil and bring it to a port in Cameroon. Switzerland, on the other hand, has almost all of the resources needed for world-class logistics, though they do face some special challenges. Geographically, they are landlocked, like Chad. Instead of being surrounded by endless dessert, Switzerland is crossed with high mountains. On the positive side, their infrastructure is probably the best in the world. They have an extensive and well-maintained network of roads, railroads, airports, and other infrastructure. In fact, they have overcome the barriers of the Alps with some of the most dramatic tunnels in the world, and the world's steepest railroad. Their institution includes all the services necessary for trade and commerce, including the famous Swiss banks. This does not mean that Switzerland is the easiest place in the world to manage logistics. They also have a heavy tax burden and laws that can make one wonder how anything gets done. Most work is forbidden on Sundays, which means trucks traveling through Europe often end up camped at the border waiting for midnight, Sunday, before they can continue their journey.

This is just an example of what to look for in comparing or assessing regions. Many firms, for example, need to decide where to locate a warehouse or enter a market. This assessment is useful at the strategic planning phase.

▶ Questions for discussion

1. Why is it necessary for logisticians to compare or assess logistics environment in different countries and regions?
2. What factors do you think should be considered to assess regional logistics environment?

▶ New specialized terms

1. cold-storage   冷藏
2. appropriately sized crane   尺寸合适的起重机
3. shortage of appropriate car   合适车皮的短缺
4. infrastructure   基础设施
5. institution   制度
6. the OPEC fund   欧佩克（石油输出国组织）基金

Case summary

两国对比：瑞士和乍得

不同国家的物流发展情况是不一样的。如果不清楚这些差异，就会出现一些情况：某个港口没有足够的冷藏仓库，缺少一定型号的起重机，或是运输有延误；某条道路尤其拥堵，某条隧道刚刚关闭，某条铁路车皮短缺。

我们可以通过比较瑞士和乍得的物流环境来认识这些差异，并考虑地理环境、基础设施和机构法律法规的影响。

乍得是非洲中部的内陆国家，运输条件很差，只有200英里全年通行的公路。人均GDP600美元，是非洲也是世界最穷的国家之一。但是乍得矿产丰富，而且有5 000万耕地。然而自20世纪80年代以来的内乱阻碍了其经济发展，现在主要靠来自世界银行、欧盟、德国、欧佩克基金和法国的资金发展。乍得计划搭设700英里的原油管线以便将储藏的9亿桶原油输送到喀麦隆的港口。而瑞士则拥有运作世界级物流的设施，尽管他们面临一些特殊的挑战，如内陆国家、山峦交错。然而瑞士的基础设施可能是世界最好的，他们有广阔和维护良好的公路网、铁路和机场等基础设施，有让人震撼的隧道和世界上坡度最大的铁路。瑞士还拥有便利贸易和商务发展的制度，其中就包括知名的瑞士银行。这并不意味着瑞士就是世界上物流运作最方便的国家：瑞士的税负很重，法律很复杂，星期日禁止大部分工作，这意味着穿越欧洲的货车需要在瑞士边境露营，过了周日午夜12点才可以继续行程。

这只是一个有关在评估和比较区域时应该注意什么的例子。例如，许多公司需要决定在何处放置仓库或进入市场。这种评估在战略规划阶段是有用的。

Hint for analysis and Reference answer

1. Why is it necessary for logisticians to compare or assess logistics environment in different countries and regions?

Adapting to the logistics differences, anticipating problems, and knowing what questions to ask at the onset of a transaction, there are no discrepancies between the expectation of a company and what can be achieved.

Take Switzerland and Chad as examples, we cannot easily come to the conclusion that Switzerland offers a better logistics environment to operate logistics activities.

2. What factors do you think should be considered to assess regional logistics environment?

Many factors should be taken into consideration when we assess the logistics environment of a certain country or region, like geography, transport-related infrastructure, institutions, bureaucracy, development of information and communication technology (ICT) etc. We can also base our assessment on the World Bank's Logistics Performance Index (LPI), which analyzes countries through six indicators:

(1) The efficiency of customs and border management clearance.

(2) The quality of trade and transport-related infrastructure.

(3) The ease of arranging competitively priced international shipments.

(4) The competence and quality of logistics services.

(5) The ability to track and trace consignments.

(6) The frequency with which shipments reach consignees within the scheduled or expected delivery time.

Part Eight

Integrated Logistics Management

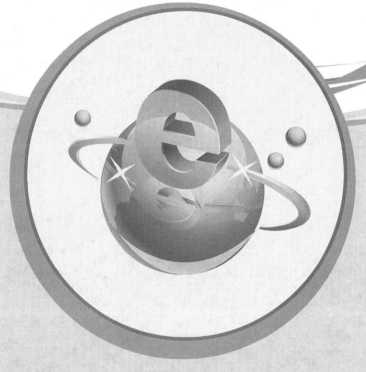

Part Eight   Integrated Logistics Management

Learning Objectives

After learning this part, you will be able to:
- Gain an understanding of the characteristics of integrated logistics
- Discuss the major activities associated with integrated logistics
- Identify and discuss the major integrated logistics interfaces within a firm
- Be familiar with service response logistics concept

Case 24

ESB

Located in California, ESB (Energetic Sports Bay) produces and distributes sportswear and running shoes. Started in the mid-1990s by Mr. Smith, the company had generated little profits because of sharp competition. In the beginning of this century, due in part to a "healthy lifestyle" campaign sweeping the United States, sales began to increase rapidly. In 2008, Mr. Smith recruited Mr. George as a logistics manager. Mr. George received his MBA degree in management science from Arkansas University and has substantial experience in the logistics field.

Currently ESB consists of five departments headed by the managers who report to the president, Mr. Smith. These departments are production, finance, marketing, logistics, and administration. Mr. Smith is glad that the departments can work cohesively and assist each other under his **democratic style of management**[1].

In the production department, there are eighty employees working at ESB's only plant, located in Los Angeles. The raw materials and parts are stored in the company warehouse near the factory. Mr. Smith believes that having a warehouse near the factory will ensure smooth operations. Finished goods transferred to a public warehouse in Austin, Texas. From there the products are delivered to the retailers.

ESB distributes its products to three major retailers. One of the three retailers, Metro Silver Plaza (MSP), holds about 60 percent of the market share. Recently MSP informed Mr. George that too many late deliveries from ESB had affected MSP's customer service levels. Mr. George said that he would cope with the matter after a **thorough investigation**[2].

ESB has about fifty raw material suppliers. Mr. Smith believes that a large supplier base is good because it encourages price competition among the suppliers and will give some competitive advantage to the company.

ESB uses a **private fleet**[3] of twenty trucks to deliver the products to its retailers' warehouses and uses the same trucks to transport products from its own site to the public warehouse.

Regarding the "late delivery issue", Mr. Smith held a conference only after a few days. He quickly met with his managers to develop a new strategy for the evolving U.S. market for the sake of protecting profitability. During the meeting, the marketing manager pointed out that to remain competitive, the company had to become a "low-cost supplier of high-quality products." The production manager argued that this is a sound idea. But he questioned how to become a low-cost supplier when the cost of raw material has arisen 15 percent because of increased raw material demand. Moreover, public warehousing cost increases had raised the delivered price of ESB's products.

Mr. George brought up the feedback from MSP about delivery failures. The administrative manager, who is responsible for the order processing and customer service, explains that the department is also responsible for employees' welfare and information processing. All middle-level managers in this department are extremely busy at dealing with **human resources affairs**[4] in the past three years.

Mr. Smith was clear that if ESB did not control the raw material cost and improve customer service, sales will continue to decline. After hearing from the managers, Smith was thinking about expanding into some emerging markets with lower labor cost. Inspired by Chinese government's "Western development strategy", Mr. Smith said he would plan to spend $200 million to set up a plant in Shannxi province (the capital is Xi'an), China. The managers believed that it is no small investment, therefore it should be studied further and carefully planned.

▶ Questions for discussion

1. How can the delivery problems to MSP be solved?
2. In your opinion, what approaches are available to ESB to becoming a highly competitive sportswear manufacturer?
3. What factors should be analyzed regarding the move to China?

▶ New specialized terms

1. democratic style of management   民主式管理风格
2. thorough investigation   彻底调查
3. private fleet   自营车队
4. human resources affair   人力资源事务

Case summary

ESB

位于美国加州的 ESB 是一家运动服饰产品制造与分销商，系史密斯先生 20 世纪 90 年代中期创办，彼时由于竞争激烈，公司利润微薄。21 世纪初随着"健康生活方式"席卷美国，公司的销售开始迅速增长。史密斯于 2008 年聘用科班出身、物流经验丰富的乔治为公司物流经理。

目前 ESB 下设五大部门，分别是生产、财务、营销、物流、行政管理。史密斯很高兴地看到，在他的民主式管理风格下，各部门能够同心同德，团结互助。

生产部有 80 名员工在 ESB 位于洛杉矶的唯一工厂工作，工厂的原料与部件储存在靠近工厂的公司自有仓库中，史密斯认为这种规划有利于公司顺畅运转。产品运往位于得克萨斯州奥斯丁的公共仓库，从那里再运往各零售商。

ESB 的产品销往三家主要的零售商，其中 MSP 占有 60%的市场份额。最近 MSP 通知乔治说，ESB 太多的延迟交货影响到了 MSP 的客户满意度，乔治答应做个全面调查后将处理此问题。

ESB 有 50 家原料供应商。史密斯认为，拥有庞大的供应商群体有利于激发供应商之间的价格战，使 ESB 获得一定的竞争优势。

ESB 拥有一支包括 20 辆卡车的运输队，既负责将产品运到零售商的仓库，也负责把产品从自己的制造厂运到公共仓库。

针对"延迟交货"问题，史密斯专门组织了一次部门经理座谈会，商谈制定新的战略，以应对激变中的美国市场，巩固盈利能力。会议中，营销部经理指出，要维持竞争优势，公司必须成为质优价廉的供应商。生产部经理认为，主意不错，但如何才能成为质优价廉的供应商呢？要知道，由于对原材料的需求上升，原材料成本已经增长了 15%，另外，公共仓储成本的上升已经推升了 ESB 产品的配送价格。

乔治汇报了来自 MSP 的有关配送失误的反馈信息。负责订单处理与客户服务的行政部的经理说，他们部门还要负责员工的福利与信息处理事务，该部门的所有中层在过去三年中一直陷入繁忙的人力资源事务而不能自拔。

史密斯意识到，如果 ESB 不能在控制原料成本的同时提高客户服务水平，销售会持续下降。听了几位部门经理的反馈后，史密斯在考虑能否在那些劳动力成本低的新兴市场国家投资建厂。他受到中国政府的"西部大开发"战略的鼓舞，计划投资 2 亿美元在中国陕西省西安市建厂。高管们认为投资数目非同小可，必须深入研究，审慎规划。

Hint for analysis and Reference answer

1. How can the delivery problems to MSP be solved?

Mr. Smith should firstly clearly distinguish the functions and responsibilities of each department. (For instance, order processing is the duty of logistics department rather than administration), then, stress timely communication with MSP, introduce EDI, JIT and Quick response system, etc. Moreover, he might redesign ESB's warehousing system and fleet or consider outsourcing its logistical business.

2. In your opinion, what approaches are available to ESB to becoming a highly competitive sportswear manufacturer?

The following measures can be effective choices:

(1) Practice JIT in material supply system

(2) Improve supplier management (keep fewer suppliers)

(3) Outsource outbound logistical activities

(4) Establish sound logistics information system

3. What factors should be analyzed regarding the move to China?

The factors are as follows:

(1) Market potential

(2) Sources of new suppliers

(3) Infrastructure—road, network, etc.

(4) Local labor cost

(5) Political and law-related difference: tax, rules, regulations, etc.

(6) Competition

(7) Culture difference: language, education, rituals, taboos, etc.

Case 25

Tastyfood

Tastyfood, established in 1976, distributes a 100-item product line of organic vegetables, fruit, condiments, and specialty items to wholesalers in several states in the eastern United States. Tastyfood introduced a policy that was designed to improve Tastyfood's service to its wholesalers and the effectiveness of the sales representatives. This program was based on two important features: (1) free sales representatives from order taking and (2) receiving orders from wholesalers on a predetermined schedule. First, the company's sales representatives were no longer to **process customer orders**[1]. Previously, they had accumulated wholesale orders until they had enough volume to make up a truckload, then they would send the orders to the head office. Under the new program, wholesalers were to e-mail their orders directly to the head office according to a fixed schedule. If they missed their fixed date, they had to wait for the next one.

These procedures were designed to increase the numbers of visits that the sales representatives could make. By eliminating the need to prepare orders, Tastyfood hoped the sales representative would spend more time determining sales patterns and the effect of **sales promotions**[2]. Under the new program, each sales representative would be more of a salesperson and less of an order taker.

Unfortunately, many wholesalers neglected to follow the predetermined order schedule. They were not accustomed to having someone tell them when to order and some object to the regimentation and lack of flexibility. Others had become dependent on the sales representative to determine what their requirements were and believed that the new program made more work for them.

If the orders did not reach Tastyfood's head office according to the schedule, the wholesaler had to wait two weeks. When a stock out occurred, the affected wholesaler could lose from 20 to 50 percent of sales of Tastyfood' products, but only Tastyfood suffered. Wholesalers and retailers carried several product lines, so when they ran out of Tastyfood brands, they simply sold other brands.

Tastyfood has no **integrated logistics department**[3] to deal with distribution activities. In the past, three sales representatives arranged transportation. When they accumulated 15,000 kilograms in orders (approaching a full truckload), they would send the orders to Tastyfood's head office for shipment. To expedite a shipment for an anxious wholesaler, a sales representative in one area would try to **pool orders**[4] with another sales representative. However, the new practice meant that the head office would ship according to the fixed schedule and arrange the shipments with the wholesalers, even if the orders totaled less than 15,000 kilograms.

Questions for discussion

1. Discuss the benefits and shortcomings of the Tastyfood system for taking orders.
2. Design a system that will provide better service to Tastyfood's customers, improve sales, and build closer ties between Tastyfood and the wholesalers.

New specialized terms

1. process customer order　处理客户订单
2. sales promotion　促销
3. integrated logistics department　整合物流部
4. pool order　集合订单

Case summary

美味食品公司

　　成立于1976年的美味食品公司在美国东部几个州经营着包含100个品类的有机蔬菜、水果、调味品和特殊产品。目前设计了一套政策旨在改进对其批发商的服务并提高销售代表的效益。这套方案基于两点考虑：一是把销售代表从接单业务中解放出来，二是让批发商按预设的时间表下订单。首先，公司的销售代表不再处理客户的订单。以前的做法是，销售代表累积的批发商订单够整车货时再把订单发到总部。新政策下，批发商按固定的日期通过电子邮件直接把订单传到总部，如果错过固定日期，批发商只能等下一次。

　　这些做法旨在增加销售代表的访问次数，让代表们有更多时间研究销售模式，提高销售效率。根据新的计划，每个销售代表会更像销售专员，而不是订单接受者。

　　然而，许多批发商忘记按固定日期下订单，一些批发商仍然依赖销售代表替他们做决定而不习惯于按固定的期限发订单，而且认为这套做法不灵活，反而给他们增加了负担。

　　一旦错过固定下单日期，批发商被迫再等两周，出现缺货的批发商会损失20%~50%的销售额。由于批发商与零售商同时销售多家供应商的产品，如果美味公司的产品缺货，他们可以转售其他品牌，因此最终受损的是美味公司。

美味公司没有整合物流部。过去,运输是由三个销售代表安排的。当他们积累了15 000千克的订单(接近一卡车),他们就会把订单送到美味公司的总部。当某个批发商发出加急订单时,销售代表之间可以临时拼单。新的制度下,即使累计订单不够15 000千克的整车发货量,总部也要按固定日期发货。

▶ Hint for analysis and Reference answer

1. Discuss the benefits and shortcomings of the Tastyfood system for taking orders.

Current system is beneficial to enhancing the performance of Tastyfood's sales representatives since they can focus on marketing and selling. Moreover, under predetermined order interval, the workload of Tastyfood's head office will be reduced and the related inventory management is relatively easy and cost effective. However, such a system is not flexible, discouraging wholesalers to sell Tastyfood's products and increase its total logistics cost in the long run.

2. Design a system that will provide better service to Tastyfood's customers, improve sales, and build closer ties between Tastyfood and the wholesalers.

Think about establishing an integrated logistics department within Tastyfood. The integrated logistics department should take charge of order processing, combined transportation, building logistics information system and customer service.

The redesigned system should be able to reinforce the CRM, pay more attention to communicate with customers, classify wholesalers and sales representatives using ABC model and promote differentiated management toward them, practice VMI for large and vital wholesalers in order to build closer ties with them, encourage sales representatives to conduct more marketing research and demand forecasting.

Case 26

Online Sales and Local Store Availability: Combining the Best of Both Worlds, or Not?

Flybai-Knight Auto (FKAuto), a major supplier of auto parts, with retail stores throughout the country, has implemented an **order online / pick up at the store**[1] option for its customers. Essentially, regular customers can shop by going to the FKAuto website and finding the items needed, submitting a web form for ordering the items, and then going to the store in a day or two to pick up the items ordered.

While similar to the conventional online ordering, or mail order process, this system involves no charge to the customer for shipping costs. The customer simply pays the same price as if she/he were to buy directly at the retail store. At the same time, orders purchased online for store pickup are filled with **stock on-hand**[2] at the store, or shipped from the nearest FKAuto distribution center if not available at the store. Benefits to the customer are the pricing that is the same as at the store and no need to wander through the store looking for items more easily found online. The downside is that items are generally not available immediately the way that normally stocked items at the store are. FKAuto benefits through strengthened customer loyalty, increased overall sales revenue, and reduced uncertainty in the demand for its goods.

This has been convenient for the customers, but it has also led to declining in-store sales. In fact, the retail outlet managers are concerned about how this **disintermediation**[3] will affect the long-term viability of their facilities. The online sales are handled completely online, to include payment via credit card, as well as sales help via live chat sessions. Thus, the retail store managers do not see the revenue associated with the online sales. At the same time, however, the handling of the shipping, storage, and pickup of those items is funded separately from normal retail store operations.

▶ Questions for discussion

1. What strategic decision is implied by the situation described for FKAuto?
2. What are the criteria for making this decision? What aspects need to be addressed to support that decision, and what data are needed to address those aspects?
3. Starting from the status quo prior to implementing the store pickup model, list the

enterprise-wide benefits associated with the new model, and what are the corresponding costs?

▶ **New specialized terms**

1. order online / pick up at the store   在线订货，门店取货
2. stock on-hand   现有存货
3. disintermediation   非居间化，绕过中介

Case summary

网上销售与当地实体店可用性：能否实现两种模式的最佳结合？

FKAuto 是一家汽车零部件供应商，其零售店遍布全国。现已推出面向顾客的"在线订货，门店取货"方案。老顾客可以从 FKAuto 的网站上搜寻与预订需要的货品，在网上提交订单后，一至两天内就可去实体店取货。

尽管与传统的在线预订或邮购流程类似，该系统却不向顾客收取运费。顾客支付的价格与直接从零售店购买的价格相同。实行"在线订货，门店取货"的订单一般在实体店都有现货，如果没有，就从最近的配送中心调运。此方案对顾客的好处是，与零售店采购价格相同，但不必亲临实体店费力搜寻所需物品。缺点在于不一定即刻就能得到所订之物。FKAuto 通过强化顾客忠诚，增加销售总收入，减少需求的不确定性而受益。

此模式在方便顾客的同时，却导致了实体店销售额的减少。事实上，零售店经理们很担心这种非居间化举措会影响到他们店面的长期生存能力。在线销售的业务处理全部线上进行，包括线上信用卡支付，现场聊天室的销售帮助等。因此零售店经理看不到与在线销售相关的收入。与此同时，网购物品的运输、储存、取货等业务所需资金却由零售店独立承担。

▶ **Hint for analysis and Reference answer**

1. What strategic decision is implied by the situation described for FKAuto?

In this case, the main strategic decision is about integrating the online and offline selling system to solve the conflicts of interest distribution between them. FKAuto needs to establish an integrated logistics department to coordinate the handling of the shipping, storage, and pickup of both online and offline ordered items.

2. What are the criteria for making this decision? What aspects need to be addressed to support that decision, and what data are needed to address those aspects?

In making this decision, FKAuto may consider customer satisfaction, economic criteria, control issues and adaptive criteria. The company needs to evaluate the total cost covering marketing, logistics and customer service, and figure out the ways to motivating retail store managers to cooperate with online sales.

The data needed to support this decision is customer responses, estimated demand of auto parts, sales performance of local retail stores, total costs of both models including marketing, logistics and customer service, etc.

3. Starting from the status quo prior to implementing the store pickup model, list the enterprise-wide benefits associated with the new model, and what are the corresponding costs?

Benefits associated with the new model are increased total sales, improved customer service, strengthened customer loyalty, reduced uncertainty in the demand for auto parts, lower information processing cost.

The corresponding costs involve management cost including team building, coordination and the design of new information system.

Part Eight Integrated Logistics Management

Case 27

Human resource management in Humanitarian Aid Supply Chains

When disasters strike, relief organizations respond by delivering aid to those in need. Their supply chains must be both fast and agile, responding to sudden onset disasters, which may occur in places as far apart as New Orleans and rural Pakistan.

Humanitarian logistics, the function that is charged with ensuring the efficient and cost-effective flow and storage of goods and materials for the purpose of alleviating the suffering of vulnerable people, came of age during the tsunami relief effort. There are clear parallels between business logistics and relief logistics, but the transfer of knowledge between the two has been limited and the latter remains relatively unsophisticated, although, more recently, greater effort has been put into understanding and developing systems that can improve the relief supply chain. Outside the world of business, logisticians in many other fields face the challenge of successfully managing the transition between **steady-state**[1] and **surge situations**[2]. This is particularly true for humanitarian logisticians preparing and executing their organizations' response to a rapid onset disaster where the price of failure can be counted in lives rather than lost profits.

For the effective functioning of a Humanitarian Logistics Organizations, it is understood that human resources play a key role. Hence, it is crucial to hire, develop and retain the "right" person at the "right" time in "right" number. Poor or non-existent training ultimately affects the quality of any operation, particularly a relief operation. The unpredictable nature of emergencies makes it difficult to retain well-trained employees, and those who have been trained are often volunteers who can only work for short periods before they must return to their "real-world" jobs. Organizations may experience as high as 80% annual **turnover**[3] in field logistics personnel, further compounding personnel issues. This results in a constant influx of untrained personnel, inexperienced in the particulars of logistics within the organization and relief as a whole.

Optimized training and minimized employee turnover can better predict performance. Some scholars illustrated the different skills and attributes that are essential in the personnel of disaster relief organizations in a T-Shaped model (see Figure 8-1). Plus, humanitarian organizations are attempting to cooperate with business logistics to offer better **logistics performance**[4].

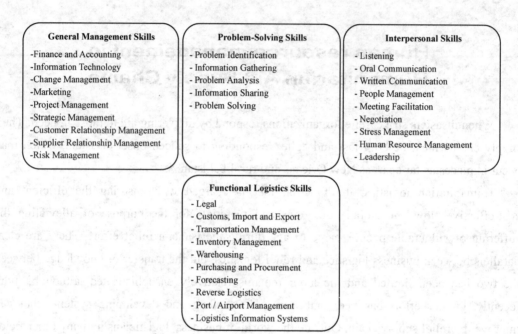

Figure 8-1　Essential skills of personnel in humanitarian organizations

Questions for discussion

1. Why is the requirement for the skills and attributes of personnel in humanitarian logistics different from that in business logistics?
2. Can you propose some shorter-range actions for human resource management of humanitarian organizations?
3. Can you propose some longer-range actions for human resource management of humanitarian organizations?

New specialized terms

1. steady-state　稳定状态的
2. surge situation　突发情况
3. turnover　流失率
4. logistics performance　物流绩效

Part Eight　Integrated Logistics Management

Case summary

人道主义援助供应链的人力资源管理

　　灾难发生时，救灾组织会提供救援，他们的供应链必须快捷，而灾难发生的地点可以是新奥尔良这样的大都市，也可以是巴基斯坦的偏僻乡村。

　　人道主义物流是为了减轻受灾人群的痛苦而对物资的高效益高效率的流动和存储，它是在海啸救济工作期间成熟起来的。企业物流和救灾物流有相同点，但是两者之间的知识转移非常有限，尽管现在已经开始重视了解和开发能改进救灾供应链的系统，救灾物流管理仍然不够成熟。除了商业领域之外，许多其他领域的物流人员时常会面临在日常情况和突发情况之间转换的挑战，这对人道主义物流人员来说尤其如此。救灾组织需要在灾难发生之处就快速反应，因为失败的代价不仅仅是利润的损失，还有生命。

　　人力资源是人道主义物流组织的有效运作的关键，因此在正确的时间以正确的数量雇佣，开发和保留正确的人是至关重要的。缺乏培训或培训不当会影响物流运作质量，尤其是救灾过程。紧急情况的不可预测性使得保留训练有素的员工很困难，而且经过培训的员工大多是志愿者，工作了一段时间以后还要返回到他们原来的工作岗位上去。一线物流人员的离职率可以高达80%，让这一情况更加严峻。这就造成一种现象：组织内和救灾过程中不断有新人流入，他们没经过专业物流知识培训，缺乏经验。

　　如果能给员工更好的培训，如果能降低员工流失率，救灾物流的绩效就会改善。有学者提出，救灾组织工作人员的技能和素质应该符合T型模型（见图8-1）。另外，一些人道主义救援组织正试图与物流实业界合作，以提供更好的物流服务。

▶ Hint for analysis and Reference answer

1. Why is the requirement for the skills and attributes of personnel in humanitarian logistics different from that in business logistics?

　　The reason is the difference between business logistics and humanitarian logistics as well as being lack of training and high turnover rate which compounded the situation.

2. Can you propose some shorter-range actions for human resource management of humanitarian organizations?

　　In the short range, humanitarian organizations can recruit people that meet the criteria in terms of general management skills, interpersonal skills and problem-solving skills.

3. Can you propose some longer-range actions for human resource management of humanitarian organizations?

　　In the longer range, humanitarian organizations can think about cooperating with business logistics and set up quick-to-get training plans.

Case 28

Fast Fashion Winner from Savvy Systems

The poor, ship-building town of La Coruña in northern Spain seems an unlikely home to a **tech-charged innovator**[1] in the fashion industry, but that's where you'll find "The Cube", the gleaming, futuristic central command of the Inditex Corporation, parent of game-changing clothes giant, Zara. The blend of technology-enabled strategy that Zara has unleashed seems to break all of the rules in the fashion industry. The firm shuns advertising, rarely runs sales, and in an industry where nearly every major player **outsources manufacturing**[2] to low-cost countries, Zara is highly vertically integrated, keeping huge swaths of its production process in-house. These counterintuitive moves are part of a recipe for success that's beating the pants off the competition, and it has turned the founder of Inditex, Amancio Ortega, into Spain's wealthiest man and the world's richest fashion executive. Zara's operations are concentrated in La Coruña and Zaragoza, Spain. A sampling of the firm's designs, and "The Cube", are shown on the firm's websites. The firm tripled in size between 1996 and 2000, then skyrocketed from $2.43 billion in 2001 to $13.6 billion in 2007. By August 2008, sales edged ahead of Gap, making Inditex the world's largest fashion retailer. While the firm supports eight brands, Zara is unquestionably the firm's crown jewel and growth engine, accounting for roughly two-thirds of sales. While competitors falter, Zara is undergoing one of the fastest global expansions the fashion world has ever seen, opening a store a day and entering new markets worldwide—68 countries so far. The chain's profitability is among the highest in the industry. Zara' clothes look like high fashion, but are comparably inexpensive. A Goldman analyst has described the chain as "Armani at moderate prices". Offering clothing lines for women, men, and children, legions of fans eagerly await "Z-day", each Zara location's twice-weekly inventory delivery that brings in the latest designs.

While overseas contract manufacturers may require hefty **lead-times**[3], trying to guess what customers want months in advance is a tricky business. For years, Gap, former industry leader, sold most of what it carried in stores. It was led by a man with a radar-right sense of style. Micky Drexler, the iconic CEO who helped turn Gap's button down shirts and khakis into America's uniform. Drexler's team had spot-on tastes throughout the 90s, but when sales declined in the early part of this decade, Drexler was left guessing on ways to revitalize the brand and he guessed wrong — disastrously wrong. Chasing the youth market, Drexler filled Gap stores with miniskirts, low-rise jeans, and even a much-ridiculed line of purple leather pants. The throngs of teenagers he sought to attract never showed up, and the shift in offerings sent Gap's mainstay customers to retailers that easily copied the styles that Gap made classic. The inventory hot potato Drexler was left with crushed the firm. Gap's same-store sales declined for 29 months straight. Profits vanished. Gap founder and Chairman Dan Fisher lamented "It took us 30 years to get to $1 billion in profits and two years to get to nothing". The firm's debt was downgraded to junk status. Drexler was out and for its new head, the board chose Paul Pressler, who shut down hundreds of stores, but the hemorrhaging continued, largely due to bad bets on colors and styles. During one holiday season, Gap's clothes were **off-target**[4] that the firm scrapped its advertising campaign and wrote off much of the inventory. The firm's model of drawing customers in via big-budget television promotion had collapsed. Pressler's tenure saw same store sales decline in 18 of 24 months.

 Conventional wisdom suggests that leveraging cheap contract labor in developing countries can keep cost-of-goods low. Firms can lower prices and sell more, or maintain higher **profit margins**[5]—all good for the bottom line. But there's an ugly downside to contract manufacturing firms that allow for the outsourcing of production. Firms that use contract manufacturers don't own the plants or directly employ the workers who produce the requested goods. Global competition among contract firms has led to race-to-the-bottom cost-cutting measures. Too often, this means that in order to have the low-cost bid, contract firms skimp on safety, ignore environmental concerns, employ child labor, and engage in other ghastly practices. Despite the fact that Gap audits contract manufacturers and has a high standard for partner conduct, the firm has repeatedly been taken to task by watchdog groups, the media, and its consumers when reports exposed unacceptable work conditions that Gap failed to catch. This includes the Oct. 2007 video showing Gap clothes made by New Delhi children as young as 10 years old in what were described as "slave labor" conditions. Gap isn't alone, Nike, Wal-Mart, and many other apparel firms have been tarnished in similar incidents. Big firms are big targets and those firms that fail to adequately ensure their products are made under acceptable labor conditions risk a brand-damaging backlash that may turn off customers, repel new hires, and leave current staff feeling betrayed.

 Having the wrong items in its stores hobbled Gap for nearly a decade, but how do you make sure stores carry the kinds of things customers want to buy? Try asking them. Zara's store managers lead the intelligence gathering effort that ultimately determines what ends up on each store's racks. Armed with handheld personal digital assistants (PDA) to gather customer input, staff regularly chat up customers to gain feedback on what they'd like to see more of. A Zara manager might casually ask: What if this skirt were in a longer length? Would you like it in a different color? What if this v-neck blouse were available in a round-neck? Another level of data gathering starts as soon as the doors close. Then the staff turns into a sort of CSI in the forensics of trend-spotting, looking for evidence in the piles of unsold items that customers tried on but didn't buy. Do there seem to be any preferences or disappointment in cloth, color, or styles offered among the products in stock? PDAs are also linked to the store's point-of-sale or **POS systems**[6]—**transaction processing systems**[7] that capture customer purchases. These systems are critical for capturing sales data, and are usually linked to inventory systems to subtract out any sold items, showing how garments rank by sales. In less than an hour, managers can send updates that combine the hard data captured at the cash register with insights on what customers would like to see. All of this valuable data allows the firm to plan styles and issue re-buy orders based on feedback rather than hunches and guesswork. The goal — to improve the frequency and quality of "sense making" for the design & planning teams.

Rather than create trends by pushing new lines via catwalk fashion shows, Zara prefers to follow with designs where there's evidence of customer demand. Data on what sells and what customers want to see goes directly to "The Cube" in La Coruña, where teams of some 300 designers crank out an astonishing 30,000 items a year versus 2,000—4,000 items offered up at big chains like H&M and Gap. While H&M has offered lines by star designers like Stella McCartney and Karl Lagerfeld, as well as celebrity collaborations with Madonna and Kylie Minogue, the Zara design staff is mostly young, hungry **Project Runway**[8] types fresh from design school. There are no prima donnas in "The Cube". Team members must be humble enough to accept feedback from colleagues, as well as share credit for winning ideas. Individual bonuses are tied to the success of the team, and teams are regularly rotated to cross-pollinate experience and encourage innovation. In the fickle world of fashion, even seemingly well-targeted designs could go out of favor in the months it takes to get plans to contract manufacturers, tool up production, then ship items to warehouses and eventually to retail locations. But getting locally targeted designs quickly onto store shelves is where Zara really excels. In one telling example, when Madonna played a set of concerts in Spain in June, 2001, teenage girls arrived to the final show sporting a Zara knock-off of the outfit she wore during her first performance. The average time for a Zara concept to go from idea to appearance in store is 15 days vs. rivals who receive new styles once or twice a season. Smaller tweaks arrive even faster. If enough customers come in and ask for, say a round neck instead of a "v" neck, a new version can be in stores within just 10 days. To put that in perspective, Zara is twelve times faster than Gap, despite offering roughly ten times more unique products! Contrast this with H&M, where it takes three to five months to go from creation to delivery — and they're considered one of the best. Other retailers need an average of six months to design a new

Part Eight   Integrated Logistics Management

collection and then another three months to manufacture it. At Zara, most of the products you see in stores didn't exist three weeks earlier, not even as sketches. The firm is able to be so responsive through a competitor-crushing combination of vertical integration. While H&M has 900 suppliers and no factories, nearly 60% of Zara's merchandise is produced in-house, with an eye on leveraging technology in those areas that speed up complex tasks, **lower cycle time**[9], and reduce error. Profits from this clothing retailer come from blending math with its data-driven fashion sense. **Inventory optimization models**[10] help the firm determine how many of which items in which sizes should be delivered to stores during twice-a-week shipments, ensuring stores are stocked with just what they need.

Outside the **distribution center**[11] in La Coruña, fabric is cut and dyed by robots in 23 highly automated factories. Zara makes 40 percent of its own fabric and purchases most of its dyes from its own subsidiary. Roughly half of the cloth arrives undyed so the firm can respond as any mid-season fashion shifts occur. After cutting and dying, many items are stitched together through a network of local cooperatives that have worked with Inditex so long they don't even operate with written contracts. The firm does leverage contract manufacturers (mostly in Turkey and Asia) to produce staple items with longer shelf lives, such as t-shirts and jeans, but this volume accounts for only about 12% of dollar volume. All of the items the firm sells end up in a 5 million square foot distribution center in La Coruña, or a similar facility in Zaragoza in Spain's northeast. The La Coruña facility is some nine times the size of Amazon's warehouse in Fernley, Nevada, or about the size of 90 football fields. The facilities move about 2.5 million items a week, with no item staying in-house for more than 72 hours. Clothes are ironed in advanced, packed on hangers, with security and price tags affixed. This means that instead of wrestling with inventory during busy periods, employees in Zara stores simply move items from shipping box to store racks, spending most of their time on **value-added functions**[12] like helping customers find what they want. Efforts like this help store staff regain as much as three hours in prime selling time. Trucks serve destinations that can be reached overnight, while chartered cargo flights serve farther destinations. The firm recently tweaked its shipping models through Air France-KLM Cargo and Emirates Air, so flights can coordinate outbound shipment of all Inditex brands with return legs loaded with raw materials and half-finished clothes items from locations outside of Spain.

Zara is also a pioneer in going green. In Fall 2007, the firm's CEO unveiled an environmental strategy that includes the use of renewable energy systems at logistics centers including the introduction of biodiesel for the firm's trucking fleet. Most products are manufactured for a **limited production run**[13]. While running out of bestsellers might be seen as a disaster at most retailers, at Zara the practice delivers several benefits. First, limited runs allow the firm to cultivate the exclusivity of its offerings. While a Gap in L.A. carries nearly the same product line as one in Milwaukee, each Zara store is stocked with items tailored to the tastes of its local clients. A Fifth Avenue shopper quips "At Gap, everything is the same", while a Zara shopper in Madrid says "you'll never end up looking like someone else". Upon visiting a Zara, the CEO of the National Retail Federation marveled "It's like you walk into a new store every two weeks". Second, limited runs encourage customers to buy right away and at full price. Savvy Zara shoppers know the newest items arrive on black plastic hangers, with store staff transferring items to wooden ones later on. Don't bother asking when something will go on sale, if you wait three weeks the item you wanted has almost certainly been sold or moved out to make room for something new. Says one 23-year old Barcelona shopper "If you see something and don't buy it, you can forget about coming back for it because it will be gone". A study by consulting firm Bain & Co. estimated that the industry average markdown ratio is approximately 50%, while Zara books some 85% of its products at full price. The constant parade of new, limited-run items also encourages customers to visit often. The average Zara customer visits the store 17 times per year, compared with only three annual visits made to competitors. Even more impressive — Zara puts up these numbers with almost no advertising. The firm's founder has referred to advertising as a "pointless distraction". The assertion carries particular weight when you consider that during Gap's collapse, the firm increased advertising spending but sales dropped. Fashion retailers spend an average of 3.5% of revenue promoting their products, while ad spending at Inditex is just 0.3%. Finally, limited production runs allows the firm to reduce to a minimum risk of making a mistake. While stores provide valuable front-line data, headquarters plays a major role in directing in-store operations. Software is used to schedule staff based on each store's forecasted sales volume, with locations staffing up, say at peak times such as lunch or early evening. The firm claims these more flexible schedules have shaved staff work hours by two percent.

  This constant refinement of operations involves the development, execution, control, maintenance, and improvement of an organization's service and manufacturing procedures throughout the firm's value chain. Definition from Porter's Value Chain has helped reverse a prior trend of costs rising faster than sales. Even the store displays are directed from "The Cube", where a basement **staging area**[14] known as "Fashion Street" houses a Potemkin village of bogus storefronts meant to mimic some of the chain's most exclusive locations throughout the world. It's here that workers test and fine-tune the chain's award-winning window displays, merchandise layout, even determine the in-store soundtrack. Every two weeks, new store layout marching orders are forwarded to managers at each location. Here's another interesting thing about Zara. Given the sophistication and level of technology integration into the firm's business processes, you'd think that Inditex would far outspend rivals on tech. But as researchers Donald Sull and Sefano Turconi discovered, "Whether measured by IT workers as a percentage of total employees or total spending as a percentage of sales, Zara's IT expenditure is less than one-fourth the fashion industry average". Zara excels by targeting technology investment at the points in its value chain where it will have the most significant impact, making sure that every dollar spend on tech has a payoff. Contrast this with high-end fashion house Prada's efforts at its flagship Manhattan location. The firm hired the Pritzker Prize-winning hipster architect, Rem Koolhaas, to design a location Prada would fill with jaw-dropping technology. All items for sale in the store would sport with **RFID**[15]—small chip-based tags that wirelessly emit a unique identifying code for the item that they are attached to. Walk into a glass dressing room and customers could turn the walls opaque, then into a sort of combination mirror and heads-up display. By wirelessly reading the tags on each garment, dressing rooms would recognize what was brought in and make recommendations of matching accessories, as well as similar products that patrons might consider. Customers could check inventory, and staff sporting PDA — handheld computing devices meant largely for mobile use outside an office setting. Examples include devices from Palm, Apple's iPhone, and devices running the Windows Pocket PC operating system. A dressing room camera would allow clients to see the front and back view side-by-side as they tried on clothes. It all sounded slick, but execution of the vision was disastrous. Customers didn't understand the foot pedals that controlled the dressing room doors and displays, with reports of some fashionistas disrobing in full view, thinking the walls went opaque when they didn't. Others got stuck in dressing rooms when pedals failed to work, or doors broke, unable to withstand the demands of the high-traffic tourist location. The inventory database was often inaccurate, regularly reporting items as out of stock even though they weren't. As for the PDAs, staff reported that they "don't really use them anymore" and that "we put them away so tourists don't play with them". The investment in Prada's in-store technology was also simply too high, with estimates suggesting the location took in just one-third the sales needed to justify expenses.

Information system is an integrated solution that combines five components: hardware, software, data, procedures, and the people who interact with and are impacted by the system. An IS also includes data used or created by the system, as well as the procedures and the people who interact with the system. Getting the right mix of these five components is critical to executing a flawless information system rollout. Financial considerations should forecast the **return-on-investment**[16], or ROI. And designers need to thoroughly test the system before deployment. At Prada's Manhattan flagship store, the effort looked like tech chosen because it seemed fashionable rather than functional. The **holy grail**[17] for the strategist is to craft a **sustainable competitive advantage**[18] that is difficult for competitors to replicate. And for nearly two decades now, Zara has delivered the goods. But that's not to say the firm is done without facing challenges. Consider the limitations of Zara's Spain-centric, **just-in-time**

manufacturing[19] model. By moving all of the firm's deliveries through just two locations, both in Spain, the firm remains hostage to anything that could create a disruption in the region. Firms often hedge risks that could shut down operations — think weather, natural disaster, terrorism, labor strife, or political unrest — by spreading facilities throughout the globe. If problems occur in northern Spain, Zara has no such fall-back. In addition to the vulnerabilities above, the model also leaves the firm potentially more susceptible to financial vulnerabilities as the euro has strengthened relative to the dollar. Many low-cost manufacturing regions have currencies that are either pegged to the dollar or have otherwise fallen against the euro. This means Zara's Spain-centric costs rise at higher rates compared to competitors, presenting a challenge in keeping profit margins in check.

As fuel costs continue to rise, the model of twice-weekly deliveries that has been key to defining the Zara experience becomes more expensive to maintain. Still, Zara is able to make up for some cost rises by increasing prices overseas (in the US, Zara items can cost 40% or more than they do in Spain). Zara reports that all North American stores are profitable, and that it can continue to grow its presence, serving 40—50 stores with just two US jet flights a week. Management has considered a logistics center in Asia, but expects current capacity will suffice until 2013. A center, say in the maquiladora region of northern Mexico, may also be able to serve the US markets via trucking capacity similar to the firm's Spain-based access to Europe, while also providing a regional center to serve growth throughout Latin America, should the firm continue its Western Hemisphere expansion.

When the economy falters, consumers simply buy less and may move a greater share of wallet to less stylish but even lower-cost offerings from deep discounters like Wal-Mart. Zara is particularly susceptible to conditions in Spain, since the market accounts for nearly 40 percent of Inditex sales. Global expansion will provide the firm with a mix of locations that may be better able to endure downturns in any single region.

The problem of sweatshop labor has plagued the clothing industry for years. Managers often feel the pressure to seek ever-lower costs and all too often end up choosing suppliers with unacceptably poor practices. Even well-meaning firms can find themselves stung by corner-cutting partners that hide practices from auditors or truck products in from unmonitored off-site locations. The results can be tragic for those exploited, and can carry lasting negative effects for the firm. Suppliers across industries now recognize that if they behave irresponsibly, the non-profit **Fair Factories Clearinghouse**[20] will carry a record of their misdeeds, notifying all members to avoid the firm. As more firms use the system, its database becomes broader and more valuable. To their credit, both Gap and Nike have joined the Fair Factories Clearinghouse. Zara has used technology to dominate the retail fashion industry as measured by sales, profitability, and growth. Excess inventory in the retail apparel industry is the kiss-of-death.

Long manufacturing lead times require executives to guess far in advance what customers will want. Guessing wrong can be disastrous. Contract manufacturing can increase profits. It also has a downside. The use of sweatshop labor and environmental abuse often associated with contract manufacturing can be a public relations nightmare if discovered and disclosed.

Questions for discussion

1. What is the "conventional wisdom" of the fashion industry with respect to design, manufacturing, and advertising?
2. What ways has Zara's model made the firm a better performer than Gap and other competitors?
3. What strategies and technologies does Zara employ to give its manufacturing and logistics operations a huge competitive edge?
4. What are the differences between Zara stores and other retail apparel stores? How these differences relate to Zara's ability to make limited production runs?
5. What risks are inherent in the conventional practices in the fashion industry? Is Zara susceptible to these risks? If so, how to prevent these risks?
6. What implications can we draw from the Zara case?

New specialized terms

1. tech-charged innovator   技术驱动的创新者
2. outsource manufacturing   制造环节的外包
3. lead-time   备货期，前置期
4. off-target   远离目标市场
5. profit margin   利润率
6. POS system   销售点系统；收款系统
7. transaction processing system   交易处理系统
8. Project Runway   T台项目角逐者
9. lower cycle time   减少周转时间
10. inventory optimization model   存货优化模型
11. distribution center   配送中心
12. value-added function   增值功能
13. limited production run   限量生产
14. staging area   暂存区，集结区
15. RFID   射频识别
16. return-on-investment（ROI）   投资收益率
17. holy grail   圣杯（梦寐以求之物）

18. sustainable competitive advantage　可持续竞争优势
19. just-in-time manufacturing　准时制生产
20. Fair Factories Clearinghouse　公正工厂数据交换中心

Case summary

以精明制胜的时装界赢家（ZARA）

在不起眼的西班牙北部造船小镇拉科鲁尼亚，你会发现一个闪耀的"立方体"大楼，这就是Inditex公司——引领潮流的服装巨人ZARA的母公司所在地。ZARA奉行的混合型技术驱动战略打破了时装界所有规则。ZARA极力缩减广告开支，很少促销，生产线高度整合，相当比例的产品由它自己的工厂来完成，而不是业界通行的转包到低成本国家。这些超常规之举是ZARA能够打败竞争对手的秘诀之一，也使得Inditex开创者阿曼西奥·奥尔特加成为西班牙首富，也是世界最富有的时装界高管。ZARA的经营集中在西班牙的拉科鲁尼亚和萨拉戈萨。该公司的设计样本和"立方体"显示在公司的网站上。ZARA自1996年至2000年业务增长了两倍，销售额从2001年的24.3亿美元猛增到2007年的136亿美元，至2008年8月，Inditex的销售额已超越Gap成为世界最大的时装零售商。ZARA是Inditex旗下八大品牌中最耀眼的品牌，销售额占集团的三分之二。在竞争对手纷纷停滞不前的时候，ZARA却在以时装界前所未有的速度向全球扩张，一天一家分店并进入世界各地的新市场，迄今已有68家。ZARA的盈利能力也是业界翘楚。ZARA的服装很新潮，但价格却不高，被Goldman的分析师誉为"价格适中的Armani"。ZARA的服装涵盖男士、女士与儿童，每个店都有大批粉丝期盼两周一次的"Z-day"，即ZARA最新款服装的上架日。

海外合同制造商需要很长的备货期，试图提前数月估测客户的需求往往十分困难。前行业领袖Gap若干年来销售的大多是店内存货。其偶像级的总裁戴克斯勒曾把Gap的领尖带纽扣的衬衫与卡其裤打造成了美国的制服。戴克斯勒的团队摸准了整个90年代的消费偏好，但是在该年代早期销售下降时，戴克斯勒还停留在探索如何复兴品牌的路上，这次他猜错了，而且是灾难性的错。为了迎合青年市场，戴克斯勒设计的Gap门店内充斥着迷你裙，低腰牛仔裤甚至颇为荒唐的一款紫色皮裤。结果他致力于吸引的青少年群体从未显现，因转换了服装却把Gap的主流客户推向了那些轻易就能模仿Gap经典款式的零售商。戴克斯勒留下的库存巨痛击倒了公司。同店销售额连续29个月下降，利润消失。Gap创始人兼主席丹·费舍尔哀叹道："奋斗三十年得到的10亿美元利润，仅两年便化为乌有。"该公司的债务被降为垃圾级。戴克斯勒只好出局，董事会任命保罗·普莱斯勒为总裁，他砍掉了数百家门店，被迫大力甩卖那些赌错颜色与款式的货品。Gap的服装注定是偏离目标市场，只好取消广告，清除大部分库存。公司试图通过大笔电视广告投入吸引顾客的模式以失败告终。普莱斯勒任期 24 个月内有 18 个月出现了同店销售额的下降。

传统思维认为，企业利用发展中国家的廉价劳动力有利于降低成本，以此薄利多销或维持高额利润。但采用合同制造的企业存在的突出弊端是他们自己没有工厂，不能直接聘用工人，只好允许生产转包。由于全球竞争激烈，转包商会竭尽全力降低成本，忽略安全与环保，雇用童工。尽管 Gap 对其合同制造商制定了严格的审查标准，也常有监督集团、媒体与自己的客户揭露其海外制造厂工作条件差、雇用童工等问题。其中包括 2007 年 10 月的一段视频，视频显示新德里 10 岁的孩子在被称为"奴隶劳工"的条件下制作 Gap 服装。耐克、沃尔玛等大牌公司也常因非法用工等被曝光，导致品牌形象受损、顾客流失、员工背叛等。

滞销服装充斥门店困扰 Gap 近十年，那么怎样才能确保所售货品正是顾客所需呢？问问顾客吧。ZARA 店长们致力于收集相关情报，最后再决定哪些服装该上架。店员手持 PDA 收集顾客资料，定期询问顾客的喜好与期盼；店长时不时地征求顾客有关服装色彩、衣领形状、长短等的意见与建议。下班后，员工们会开展类似"犯罪现场调查"式的另类信息收集，探寻顾客试穿而未买货品之原因。在库存商品中，布料、颜色或款式是否有让人喜爱或失望的地方。ZARA 的 PDA 直接连到店内的 POS 机上，这些交易处理系统对于获取销售数据十分关键，再与库存系统连接就能方便掌握服装销量排名情况。不到一个小时，店长就能把融合了收款机获取的实际数据与反映顾客期望的灵感类信息传到总部。所有这些有价值的数据促使该企业进行基于反馈的款式规划与订单下达而不是凭直觉或猜测。目的是提高其设计与规划团队"感应市场"的频率与质量。

相比于通过 T 台秀推出新系列来引领潮流，ZARA 更喜欢追随那些有消费者需求证据的设计。销售与反映顾客期望的数据直接传到拉科鲁尼亚的"立方体"中心，在那里 300 多人构成的设计团队每年能快速推出 30 000 个服装款式，超过 H&M 与 Gap 的 2 000~4 000 个的水平。与 H&M 动辄聘请明星设计师和麦当娜之类的明星宣传不同，ZARA 的设计师大多是年轻的、设计学校毕业不久的 T 台项目角逐者，没有大牌明星。设计师必须乐于接受同行建议并分享成功的创意。个人奖金与团队的成功与否直接挂钩，各个设计团队要经常轮换，互相传经，鼓励创新。在变化无常的时装界，即使看上去定位准确的设计，在经历签约制作，缝制，运回仓库直至门店后也会过时。ZARA 真正出色之处是把迎合当地顾客的设计理念快速推上货架。一个典型的例子是，2001 年 6 月，麦当娜到西班牙举行演唱会，在最后一场演出时，人们就看到了青春少女们穿上了仿制版的麦当娜首演套装。从概念到服装摆上门店货架，ZARA 只需要 15 天，而竞争对手门店内一个季度只能展示一到两次新款。ZARA 推出的独特新品是 Gap 的 10 倍，而上市速度比之快 12 倍。H&M 的产品从创意到上架需要 3 到 5 个月，这还算较优秀的，其他零售商设计一个新款就要 6 个月，再生产出来又需要 3 个月！而 ZARA 店内销售的货品大多不超过 3 周，3 周前甚至连草图都没有。ZARA 能够通过综合的垂直整合策略挤压竞争对手并对市场做出快速的反应。H&M 有 900 家供应商，没有工厂，而 ZARA 近 60%的商品是自己生产的，公司着眼于利用这些领域的技术来加快完成复杂任务，减小周转时间和降低误差。该服装零售商的利润源于将数学与数据驱动的时尚意识紧密融合。例如，各种库存优化模型帮助公司制定一周两次的门店送货决策：选择哪个货品？哪个款式？该送多少？以此保证每个门店储存的都是顾客需要的。

在拉科鲁尼亚的配送中心，ZARA 拥有 23 家由机器人剪裁与染色的高度自动化的布料加工厂，公司 40%的布料由自己生产，所需的染料大部分从自己集团下属的厂家购买。送来的布料中有 50%是未染色的，这样就可以迅速应对夏季颜色变换的潮流。裁剪好的布料被运送到由一些当地合作工厂组成的制作网络中进行缝合。这些工厂与 Inditex 合作多年，几乎不用签订书面合同便能完成任务。该公司也利用转包商（多数在土耳其和亚洲）生产那些货架周期稍长的稳销品，如 T 恤与牛仔服，但销售额仅占 12%。公司销售的所有货品都源于拉科鲁尼亚的占地五百万平方英尺，相当于 90 个足球场大的配送中心或位于西班牙西北部的萨拉戈萨的类似设施。在这些场地一周运出 250 万件物资，没有一件物品储存超过 72 小时。服装事先熨好，挂上衣架，附上安全标识与价签，经过专用设备分拣装箱，被昼夜服务的包裹物流商运往各门店的暂存区。这意味着 ZARA 的店员在销售高峰期不用打理库存，只需把运输箱搬上货架，从而将大半时间用于处理增值活动，如帮助顾客寻找商品，像这样的努力帮助店员获得 3 个小时的黄金销售时间。一夜可以到达的门店用卡车运输，更远一些的使用货运班机。公司最近调整了运输模式，租用法荷联合航空集团与阿联酋航空的货运服务，以便协调所有 Inditex 旗下产品的外埠运输与西班牙之外的原材料与半成品服装的回程运输。

ZARA 在绿色经营方面，也走在同行前列。2007 年秋，公司总裁宣布了一项环保战略，即在物流中心使用再生能源（运输车队引入生物燃料）。ZARA 的多数产品采用"限量生产"。对于大多数服装商店来说，最热销的商品断货意味着一场灾难，但 ZARA 鼓励暂时的缺货，从而产生若干好处。首先，限量能够培养产品的唯一性。Gap 的洛杉矶分店与密尔沃基分店所售服装几乎一模一样，而 ZARA 的货品总是能够迎合当地顾客的口味。位于纽约第五大道的 ZARA 专卖店的顾客嘲弄说："在 Gap 的店里，东西都是千篇一律。"马德里 ZARA 的一位常客说，"到最后，你永远都不会跟别人穿得一样。"全国零售联合会的总裁参观 ZARA 时曾惊叹道："每隔两周你走进的都是面貌一新的门店。"其次，限量生产能够鼓励顾客立刻购买，而且不必打折。精明的 ZARA 顾客都知道最新款的服装都挂在黑色的塑料衣架上，后来店员再把它们移到木头衣架上。不必费心去问哪件衣服何时搞促销，如果你等上 3 个星期，很可能就售罄了或让位给新款服装了。"如果你看到了一件衣服却没买，就把它忘了吧，不用指望以后再来，因为以后就买不到了。"巴塞罗那一位 23 岁的顾客如此说道。咨询公司 Bain 的研究估计，时装业的平均折价率大约 50%，而 ZARA 85%的商品能够按原价售出。限量版的新款服装频频上架也鼓励顾客经常惠顾。ZARA 的顾客每年平均光顾 17 次，而竞争对手每年只有 3 次。更让人印象深刻的是，ZARA 取得这样的成绩却几乎不打广告。公司的创始人曾将广告称为"毫无意义的干扰"。Gap 在崩溃期间，虽然增加了广告支出但销售额下降了，这正应验了上述论断。Inditex 集团广告费用只占销售额的 0.3%，而时装零售商的这一比例平均为 3.5%。最后，限量生产有利于公司降低犯错的风险。门店提供高价值的前台数据的同时，总部在引导店面经营方面发挥了主导作用。基于每个门店提供的销量预测数据，电脑软件帮助规划店员的作息时间，比如，有的店可能在午餐或夜幕刚降临的时候需要增加店员。公司认为这种更加灵活的时间表把店员的工作时间缩减了 2%。

这种运营的不断完善，涉及贯穿公司价值链的一个组织的服务和制造程序的开发、执行、控制、维护和改进。波特价值链的定义有助于扭转以前成本上升速度快于销售的趋势。即使是店面陈列也来自"立方体"的导引，其中被称为"时尚街"的地下室暂存区设有 Potemkin 村庄的仿造店面，旨在模仿世界各地一些连锁店最独特的环境。正是在这里，工人们测试并调整了连锁店屡获殊荣的橱窗商品布局，甚至确定了店内配乐。每隔两周，商店布局的新指令将转发给每个门店的经理。鉴于公司通过技术整合其业务流程达到的高级水平，人们会认为 Inditex 在技术方面的投资远远超过竞争对手。但正如研究人员 Donald Sull 和 Sefano Turconi 所发现的那样，"无论是 IT 员工在员工总数中的百分比还是总支出占销售额的百分比，ZARA 的 IT 支出都不到时尚行业平均水平的四分之一"。ZARA 擅长将价值链中的技术投资定位于其最重要的效力点，确保每一美元的技术支出都能带来回报。这与高端时装品牌普拉达（Prada）在曼哈顿旗舰店的煞费苦心形成鲜明对比。该公司聘请了普利兹克奖得主——当红建筑师雷姆库尔哈斯（Rem Koolhaas）采用了令人印象深刻的技术设计店面。商店中出售的所有商品都使用基于射频识别技术的小型芯片标签，这些标签能够以无线方式为其所附的物品发出唯一的识别码。走进玻璃更衣室，顾客可以将墙壁变得不透明，然后变成一种组合镜子和平视显示器。通过无线读取每件衣服上的标签，更衣室将识别所带进来的东西，并提供匹配配件的建议，以及顾客可能考虑的类似产品。客户可以查看库存，员工则手持用于办公室外移动使用的 PDA 计算设备，可以展示在包括 Palm，Apple 的 iPhone 和运行 Windows Pocket PC 操作系统的设备上。更衣室相机允许客户在试穿衣服时并排看到前后视图。这一切听起来很动人，但将愿景变为现实会招致灾难性后果。客户并不清楚控制更衣室的门和显示器的脚踏板，有报道称一些时尚人士在试衣时走光了。当踏板无法工作时，有顾客被困在更衣室，或门坏了，应付不了旅游景点高峰客户流的需求。库存数据库通常不准确，有时会把缺货的物品显示为有货。至于 PDA，工作人员报告称他们"不再使用它们"，并且"我们把它们放在一边，以免游客们拿去把玩"。普拉达店内的技术设施投资的确过高，估计此类成本占到该店销售额的三分之一。

信息系统则是一个集成的解决方案，它结合了五个组件：硬件、软件、数据、程序以及与系统交互并受系统影响的人员。获得这五个组件的正确组合对于实施完美的信息系统部署至关重要。从财务方面考虑，则应该预测投资回报率。设计人员需要在部署之前彻底测试系统。在 Prada 的曼哈顿旗舰店，这种努力看起来是基于科技导向，但实际上华而不实。战略制定者的至高目标是创造竞争者难以复制的可持续竞争优势。近二十年来，ZARA 达到了这个目的。但这并不是说公司没有面临新挑战。考虑一下 ZARA 以西班牙为中心的即时制造模式的局限性：仅通过西班牙的两个地点配送公司的所有货物，该公司将受制于可能造成该地区中断的任何事件。企业通常会通过全球布局设施网点对冲运营失败的风险（想一想天气，自然灾害，恐怖主义，劳资纠纷或政治动荡吧）。如果西班牙北部出现问题，ZARA 就没有这种退路。除了上述漏洞之外，由于欧元相对于美元走强，此模式还使公司更容易受到金融波动的影响。许多低成本制造业区域的货币与美元挂钩或者相对于欧元贬值。这意味着与竞争对手相比，ZARA 以西班牙为中心的成本会上升更快，这对于维持原有利润率提出了挑战。

虽有燃料成本持续上升，保持一周两次送货的模式变得日益昂贵，然而，ZARA 还是可以通过提高海外价格来弥补一些上涨的成本（在美国，ZARA 产品的售价比西班牙高出 40%或更多）。ZARA 报告说，所有北美商店都有盈利，而且它可以继续维持局面，每周只用两架喷气式飞机服务美国的 40-50 家商店。管理层已考虑在亚洲建立一个物流中心，但预计目前的产能将足够持续到 2013 年。在墨西哥北部的保税加工厂设立一个中心也可能通过类似于西班牙到达欧洲的卡车运输服务于美国市场，如果该公司继续其西半球的扩张，该中心还可以服务于整个拉丁美洲业务增长的需要。

当经济不景气时，消费者只需减少购买量，并可能花更多的钱购买沃尔玛等深层折扣店的时尚但成本更低的产品。ZARA 特别容易受到西班牙当地条件的影响，因为该市场占 Inditex 销售额的近 40%。全球扩张将为公司提供多个地点，可以更好地承受单一地区的经济衰退。

血汗工厂的劳动力问题多年来一直困扰着服装业。管理人员经常感受到寻求不断降低成本的压力，并且往往最终选择那些不良经营的供应商。即使是善意的公司也会受到"黑心"伙伴的拖累，这些伙伴想法逃避审查或者从不受监控的场外据点非法运货。对于那些受牵连的公司来说，结局可能是悲惨的，甚至可能给公司带来持久的负面影响。各个行业的供应商现在都认识到，如果他们的行为不负责任，非盈利的公平工厂信息交换中心将记录他们的不当行为，通知所有成员避开该公司。随着越来越多的公司使用该系统，其数据库变得更广泛，更有价值。值得赞扬的是，Gap 和 Nike 都加入了公平工厂信息交换中心。根据销售额，盈利能力和增长情况衡量，ZARA 已经通过先进技术主宰了零售时尚产业。服装零售行业的过剩库存无异于自取灭亡。长的制造交货期要求主管们提前猜测客户需求，如果猜错就可能带来灾难性的后果。制造外包可能增加利润，但也有不利的一面。通常与制造外包相关的雇佣血汗工厂的劳动力和糟蹋环境的行为，一旦被发现并曝光，很可能就是公司公关的噩梦到来之时。

▷ Hint for analysis and Reference answer

1. What is the "conventional wisdom" of the fashion industry with respect to design, manufacturing, and advertising?

According to conventional wisdom, leveraging cheap contract labor in developing countries can reduce production cost. Firms outsourcing their manufacturing in developing countries can lower prices and sell more, or maintain higher profit margins. Most fashion retailers like Gap, H&M place orders for a seasonal collection before these lines make appearance in stores. Since overseas contract manufacturers normally require longer lead-times, these retailers tend to guess what customers' wants and preference months in advance. Besides, they are willing to create trends by pushing new lines via catwalk fashion shows and offer those lines by star designers.

Under such "conventional wisdom," advertising plays an important role in increasing brand awareness of consumer goods like clothing. Fashion retailers spend an average of 3.5% of revenue promoting their products.

2. What ways has Zara's model made the firm a better performer than Gap and other competitors?

Closely follow fashion trends, frequently updating clothing styles and offering customers with more variety all contribute to the unique attractiveness of Zara and the ensuing customers' preference and loyalty to it. Advanced technology also helps Zara identify and manufacture the clothes customers want, get those products to market quickly, and eliminate costs related to advertising, inventory management, etc.

3. What strategies and technologies does Zara employ to give its manufacturing and logistics operations a huge competitive edge?

Zara's combination of vertical integration and technology-orchestrated supplier coordination, just-in-time manufacturing, and efficient logistics system allows it to go from design to shelf in much shorter period than its rivals. The technologies Zara has employed include Bar code, Optical identification, PDAs and POS systems, inventory optimization model, ERP, CAD/CAM, CRM and ICT platform.

4. What are the differences between Zara stores and other retail apparel stores? How these differences relate to Zara's ability to make limited production runs?

More styles, closer to young fashion-seekers, smaller batch and faster delivery are the main differences between Zara stores and other retail apparel stores.

Limited fashion stock and frequently running out of bestsellers allow Zara to cultivate the exclusivity of its offerings. Each Zara store is stocked with items tailored to the tastes of its local clients. While stores provide valuable front-line data, headquarters plays a major role in directing in-store operations. Software is used to schedule staff based on each store's forecasted sales volume, with locations staffing up, say at peak times such as lunch or early evening. All these are connected with Zara's strategy of limited production runs.

5. What risks are inherent in the conventional practices in the fashion industry? Is Zara susceptible to these risks? If so, how to prevent these risks?

There are financial risks, information risks and law risks.

Zara is susceptible to these risks. Though Zara's operation model is difficult to copy, its management must continually scan its environment for new threats and opportunities, and be prepared to instantly move on them with new strategies and state-of-the-art technologies in order to prevent these risks.

6. What implications can we draw from the Zara case?

Owing to the timeliness and seasonality of fashion product, costume firms have to get high-efficient information feedback and respond to customers quickly in order to survive and grow in this increasingly fierce market. Chinese firms must break up conventional wisdom, integrate material supply, manufacturing and product distribution into an entire efficient supply chain under which information sharing is fully realized.

A strategist must always scan the state of the market as well as state-of-the-art in technology, looking for new opportunities and remaining aware of impending threats.

In fashion industry, the close combination of IT and business process play a vital role in building a firm's strength. Therefore, Chinese firms should pay more attention to technology-orchestrated vertical integration through sound supplier coordination, just-in-time manufacturing, and efficient logistics system. Only in this way can firms forge a quick-response mechanism characterized as "purchasing based on production, production based on customer demand".

Part Eight Integrated Logistics Management

Case 29

LIDL Sweden

The company of Lidl was founded in 1930 in Germany as a grocery and the first retailing store was opened in 1973, followed by a global expansion during 1990s. The company is established in most part of Europe, with approximately 10,000 stores in nearly 30 countries.

The first Lidl retailing store was opened in Sweden in 2003, and Lidl today distributes 178 stores from south to north Sweden, with about 4,000 employees. The headquarter of Lidl Sweden is based in Solna, and the company has two central stocks in Halmstad and Rosersberg. One thing worth to mention is that Lidl claims to have the world's greenest new trading building as part of their logistic systems. Sweden is one of Lidl's best growing market as it is planning to open a new headquarters in Barkarby city in 2019, and a new warehouse in Örebro will be operational in 2019.

Logistics and supply chain planning of Lidl Sweden

Lidl claim themselves as "choose to live a little". According to the summarized sentence of their manager, they "want to offer top quality goods and services at the best price. We do this by working smart and long-term sustainability." Since Lidl has a low-price strategy and the stores are simply designed, customers can therefore merely pay for what they get in their grocery blankets. It seems that though Lidl explains that they are selling high quality products, they actually pay more value and effort to achieve low price. The company takes various methods as business model to reduce their expenses. Direct purchases from producers helps to avoid additional agent charges and provides full control over the food quality. Optimized distribution through the volume and distance contributes to reduce environmental harm and save funds as well as raise sustainability, with commitment to saving natural resources by reducing consumption of electricity and using better types of diesel.

The structure of Lidl's logistics system consists of stock, transportation, and recycling. So, the whole supply chain starts from warehouse, as purchasing and manufacturing is taken over by its suppliers.

Lidl has its **cross-stocking center**[1] in Germany and the national distribution directly to the warehouse. For Lidl, warehousing includes all aspects of operations that have a relationship to productivity, warehouse layouts, and general systems. The supply chain management is divided into two distinct departments. For supply chain, the department aided by regional parts focusing on availability, **write-off control**[2] and freshness of product. In the layout management part, the primary responsibilities consist of all forms of product placing and storing and generating the operational instructions. At Lidl, the supply chain does not reach the end when the item is physically delivered to the store, since in layout management it is ensured that each product placement is designed referring to maintain simplicity and improve efficiency, while delivering obvious message to customers.

The store is linked to a central warehouse (geographically divided). All goods flow to shop is via the central warehouse, 1 delivery per day, 7 days a week; 1 contact point for all orders. A perfect example for the last new techniques and innovation contributing to Lidl's transportation is its new truck. Lidl partnered with a Stockholm-based **start-up company**[3] named as Einride to run a new type of truck called T-Pod which is a driverless and **emission-free cargo truck**[4] followed by the plans to pilot the new remote-control delivery system.

During the year of 2016-2017, Lidl managed to completely switch to alternative fuels such as electricity, natural gas, biodiesel, or eco-labeled diesel, which is shown by its data to have decreased the environmental impact by 26 percent. According to Johannes Fieber, CEO of Lidl Sweden, Einride's self-driving T-pod is "a big step forward in Lidl's battle for fossil free transport".

Recycling is an important part of the Lidl's logistics system since as an international company it is paying an immense stress on the environmental responsibility and actively recycle and lowing waste to reduce materials and to reuse the resources.

Cost components in logistics and transportation of Lidl Sweden

According to its department head Carl Ceder, Lidl' logistics costs are divided into three categories: fix costs, variable costs and a diesel rider to adapt to fluctuations in diesel price.

Fix costs are by far the largest category, where the costs for the truck and the wages of the driver as well as insurance etc. are included. Variable costs consist of "wear and tear" costs including the basic costs for diesel. In Lidl's transportation, 52% of diesel is HVO / RME (biodiesel) or LNG (biogas), 44% is Swan-labeled diesel, and other 4% is Einride Trucks.

The main **KPIs**[5] (Key performance indicator) that Lidl Sweden are monitoring in regard to transport could be concluded as:

- Transport costs as % of store turnover;
- Cost per delivered EP (unit of measurement by Lidl);
- EP per truck shift;
- Truck shift utilization-truck using hours;
- Fill-rate / utilization of the truck;
- Kilometer per delivered EP.

Here, the data of transport costs as % of store turnover, cost per delivered EP (namely transport costs / delivered EP for the period) should be gathered in situation both with and without diesel to reach a grounded analysis as considering the main cost components sorts mentioned before. The EP per truck shift could be interpreted as how many EP can we deliver per paid shift, while the Fill-rate / utilization of the truck is digitalized by how well are the floor space of the vehicle filled up and truck using hours.

Questions for discussion

1. What are Lidl Sweden's logistical strengths and weaknesses?
2. How can Lidl Sweden improve its logistical operations?
3. What are the potential problems facing Lidl Sweden in its future development? How to solve these problems?

New specialized terms

1. cross-stocking center   直接换装中心
2. write-off control   核销控制
3. start-up company   初创公司
4. emission-free cargo truck   无排放的货车
5. KPI   关键绩效指标

Case summary

Lidl 瑞典公司

Lidl 公司于 1930 年在德国成立，第一家零售店于 1973 年开业，随后在 20 世纪 90 年代开展全球扩张。该公司在欧洲大部分地区设立分部，在近 30 个国家拥有约 1 万家门店。

瑞典的第一家 Lidl 零售店于 2003 年开业。今日，Lidl 在瑞典全境共有 178 家店铺，员工约 4 000 人。瑞典 Lidl 总部位于索尔纳，该公司在哈尔姆斯塔德和罗斯伯格拥有两个中央仓储区。值得一提的是，Lidl 声称将打造世界上最环保的新贸易大楼作为其物流系统的一部分。瑞典是 Lidl 发展最快的市场之一，因为它计划于 2019 年在 Barkarby 开设一个新总部，而在 Örebro 的新仓库也将于 2019 年底投入运营。

Lidl 瑞典公司的物流和供应链系统

Lidl 的宗旨是"希望以最优惠的价格提供最优质的商品和服务。我们通过智能化和长期可持续性来实现这一目标。"由于 Lidl 采用低价策略并且商店设计简单，虽然 Lidl 解释说他们销售的是高质量的产品，但实际上他们付出了更多的价值和努力来实现低价格。公司采用各种模式化的方法，以减少开支——从生产者直接购买有助于避免额外的代理费用，并全方位控制食品质量；通过运量和运距的优化配送有助于减少环境危害并节省资金、提高可持续性；Lidl 同时还致力于通过减少电力消耗和使用更好的柴油来节约自然资源。

Lidl 物流系统包括三个功能：库存、运输和回收。整个供应链是从仓库开始的，采购和制造直接由供应商接管。

Lidl 在德国设有直接转运中心，在全国范围内将物资直接配送到仓库。对于 Lidl 来说，仓储包括与生产力、仓库布局和一般系统相关的所有操作。供应链管理则分为两个不同的部门——对于供应链本身，该部门在地区分部的帮助下，重点关注可得性、核销控制和产品的新鲜度；在布局管理部分，其主要职责包括放置和存储各种产品以及生成操作指令。物品被运送到门店并不是供应链的终点，因为在布局管理中，还须确保每个产品放置的设计都保持了简单性，以提高效率同时向客户传递明确的信息。

商店与一个中央仓库相连（地理上分开）。所有货物都是通过中央仓库流向商店，每天 1 次，每周 7 天，所有订单都有一个联络点。

在技术方面，Lidl 运输技术创新的一个完美例子是它的新型卡车。Lidl 与一家名为 Einride 的斯德哥尔摩创业公司合作，运营一种名为 T-Pod 的新型卡车，这是一种无人驾驶且零排放的货运卡车，随后计划推出新的远程控制输送系统。在 2016—2017 年期间，Lidl 设法完全转向替代燃料，如电力，天然气，生物柴油或生态柴油。数据显示，此举将环境危害减少了 26%。根据瑞典 Lidl 首席执行官约翰内斯菲伯的说法，Einride 的自动驾驶 T-pod 是"Lidl 向无化石燃料运输奋斗中的一大进步"。循环利用是 Lidl 物流系统的重要组成部分，其作为一家国际公司，特别重视承担环境责任，并积极回收和减少废物，以降低材料消耗和重复利用资源。

Lidl 瑞典公司物流和运输的成本要素

根据其部门主管卡尔·赛德的说法，Lidl 的物流成本分为三类：固定成本、可变成本和适应价格波动的柴油附加费。

固定成本最高，包括卡车的成本和司机的工资以及保险等。可变成本则包括耗油之类的"磨损"成本。在 Lidl 的运输中，52%的柴油是 HVO/RME（生物柴油）或 LNG（沼气），44%是天鹅牌的柴油，另外 4%是 Einride Trucks。

Lidl 瑞典在运输方面监控的主要关键绩效指标可归结为：

- 运输成本占商店营业额的百分比；
- 每次交付一个 EP（Lidl 采用的计量单位）的成本；
- 每班次卡车的 EP；
- 卡车的轮班使用率——卡车使用时间；
- 卡车的满载率/利用率；
- 每次交付 EP 的公里数。

在这里，运输成本的数据占门店营业额的百分比，每个交付的 EP 的成本（即运输成本/交付期间的 EP）应该在有和没有柴油的情况下收集，以便在考虑主要成本构成时达到基础分析之前提到的水准。每个卡车班次的 EP 可以解释为每个付费班次我们可以送达多少 EP，而卡车的满载率/利用率是车厢填满程度与卡车使用时间的数量化。

Hint for analysis and Reference answer

1. What are Lidl Sweden's logistical strengths and weaknesses?

Lidl Sweden's main logistical strengths are as follows.

(1) Experience: Lidl Sweden already has almost a decade local experience.

(2) Competitive price with developed cost-control system.

(3) Already habituated recycling strategies such as returned goods and recyclable materials are collected by delivery truck and "Download-self" transport on the way back.

(4) Collaboration between organizations and companies such as Stockholm City, KTH, Svebol Logistics, Volvo.

Lidl Sweden's main logistical weaknesses are as follows.

(1) Quality of product being questioned.

(2) Being complained about lack of qualified environment labeling, ineffective transportation, and misleading advertisement.

(3) A limited market share in Sweden.

2. How can Lidl Sweden improve its logistical operations?

Lidl Sweden might improve its logistical operations through the following approaches:

(1) Developing and improving shipping and storage processes.

(2) Conducting cost-control projects within each area.

(3) General cost monitoring and analysis.

(4) Testing and evaluating new flows and techniques.

3. What are the potential problems facing Lidl Sweden in its future development? How to solve these problems?

Main problems facing Lidl Sweden are growing labor cost such as driver wages due to a lack of drivers and the rising price of HVO bio diesel.

Lidl Sweden might exploit some new techniques such as non-driver driving, digital storage and AI management to solve those problems. Off-peak project and optimization of transport plans are also helpful tools in overcoming potential barriers.

Appendix

A Guide to Case Analysis and Case Discussion

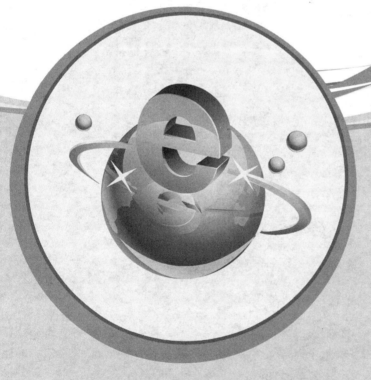

Appendix   A Guide to Case Analysis and Case Discussion

Part One   Objectives of Case Analysis

Using cases to learn about the practice of management is a powerful way for you to realize the following objectives.

1. Increase your understanding of what managers should and should not do in guiding a business to success.

2. Build your skills in assessing a firm's resource strengths and weaknesses and in conducting strategic and operational analysis in a variety of industries and competitive situations.

3. Get valuable practice in identifying managerial issues that need to be addressed, evaluating strategic alternatives, and formulating workable plans of action.

4. Enhance your sense of business judgment, as opposed to uncritically accepting the authoritative ideas or suggested answers.

5. Gaining in-depth exposure to different industries and companies, thereby acquiring something close to actual business experience.

Case discussions usually produce good arguments for more than one course of action. Differences of opinion nearly always exist. Thus, should a class discussion conclude without a strong, unambiguous consensus on what do to, don't complain too much when you are not told what the answer is or what the company actually did. Just remember that in the business world answers don't come in conclusive black-and-white terms. There are nearly always several feasible courses of action and approaches, each of which may work out satisfactorily. Moreover, in the business world, when one elects a particular course of action, there is no peeking at the back of a book to see if you have chosen the best thing to do and no one to turn to for a demonstrably correct answer.

Hence, the important thing for you to understand about analyzing cases is that the managerial exercise of identifying, diagnosing, and recommending is aimed at building your skills of business judgment. Discovering what the company actually did is no more than frosting on the cake — the actions that company managers actually took may or may not be "right" or best (unless there is accompanying evidence that the results of their actions were highly positive).

The purpose of giving you a case assignment is not to cause you to run to the library or surf the internet to discover what the company actually did but, rather, to enhance your skills in sizing up situations and developing your managerial judgment about what needs to be done and how to do it. The aim of case analysis is for you to become actively engaged in diagnosing the business issues and managerial problems posed in the case, to propose workable solutions, and to explain and defend your assessments—this is how cases provide you with meaningful practice at being a manager.

Part Two How to prepare a Case for Class Discussion

If this is your first experience with the case method, you may have to reorient your study habits. Unlike lecture courses where you can get by without preparing intensively for each class and where you have latitude to work assigned readings and reviews of lecture notes into your schedule, a case assignment requires conscientious preparation before class. You will not get much out of hearing the class discuss a case you haven't read, and you certainly won't be able to contribute anything yourself to the discussion. What you have got to do to get ready for class discussion of a case is to study the case, reflect carefully on the situation presented, and develop some reasonable thoughts. Your goal in preparing the case should be to end up with what you think is a sound, well-supported analysis of the situation and a sound, defensible set of recommendations about which managerial actions need to be taken.

To prepare a case for class discussion, we suggest the following approach:

1. Skim the case rather quickly to get an overview of the situation it presents. This quick overview should give you the general flavor of the situation and indicate the kinds of issues and problems that you will need to wrestle with. If your instructor has provided you with study questions for the case, now is the time to read them carefully.

2. Read the case thoroughly to digest the facts and circumstances. During this reading, try to gain full command of the situation presented in the case. Begin to develop some tentative answers to the study questions your instructor has provided or that are provided in the case book. If your instructor has elected not to give you assignment questions, then start forming your own picture of the overall situation being described.

3. Carefully review all the information presented in the exhibits. Often, there is an important story in the numbers contained in the exhibits. Expect the information in the case exhibits to be crucial enough to materially affect your diagnosis of the situation.

4. Decide what the strategic issues are. Until you have identified the strategic issues and problems in the case, you don't know what to analyze, which tools and analytical techniques are called for, or otherwise how to proceed. At times the strategic issues are clear — either being stated in the case or else obvious from reading the case. At other times you will have to dig them out from all the information given; if so, the study questions and the hints following selected questions will guide you.

5. Apply the concepts and techniques of managerial analysis you have been studying. Managerial analysis is not just a collection of opinions; rather, it entails applying the concepts

and analytical tools described in textbook to cut beneath the surface and produce sharp insight and understanding. Every case assigned is management related and presents you with an opportunity to usefully apply what you have learned. Your instructor is looking for you to demonstrate that you know how and when to use the material presented in the text chapters.

6. Check out conflicting opinions and make some judgments about the validity of all the data and information provided. On many occasions, cases report views and contradictory opinions. Forcing you to evaluate the data and information presented in the case helps you develop your powers of inference and judgment. Asking you to resolve conflicting information "comes with the territory" because a great many managerial situations entail opposing points of view, conflicting trends, and sketchy information.

7. Support your diagnosis and opinions with reasons and evidence. The most important things to prepare for are your answers to the question "Why?" For instance, if after studying the case you are of the opinion that the company's managers are doing a poor job, then it is your answer to "Why?" that establishes just how good your analysis of the situation is. If your instructor has provided you with specific study questions for the case, by all means prepare answers that include all the reasons and number-crunching evidence you can muster to support your diagnosis.

8. Develop an appropriate action plan and set of recommendations. Diagnosis divorced from corrective action is sterile. The test of a manager is always to convert sound analysis into sound actions — actions that will produce the desired results. Hence, the final and most telling step in preparing a case is to develop an action agenda for management that lays out a set of specific recommendations on what to do. Bear in mind that proposing realistic, workable solutions is far preferable to casually tossing out off-the-top-of-your-head suggestions. Be prepared to argue why your recommendations are more attractive than other courses of action that are open.

As long as you are conscientious in preparing your analysis and recommendations, and have ample reasons, evidence, and arguments to support your views, you shouldn't fret unduly about whether what you've prepared is "the right answer" to the case. In case analysis there is rarely just one right approach or set of recommendations. Managing companies are not such exact sciences that there exists a single provably correct analysis and action plan for each managerial situation. Of course, some analyses and action plans are better than others; but, in truth, there's nearly always more than one good way to analyze a situation and more than one good plan of action. So, if you have carefully prepared the case by developing your own answers to the assignment questions for the case, don't lose confidence in the correctness of your work and judgment.

Part Three   How to participate in Class Discussion of a Case

Classroom discussions of cases are sharply different from attending a lecture class. In a case class, students do most of the talking. The instructor's role is to solicit student participation, keep the discussion on track, ask "Why?" often, offer alternative views, play the devil's advocate (if no students jump in to offer opposing views), and otherwise lead the discussion. The students in the class carry the burden for analyzing the situation and for being prepared to present and defend their diagnoses and recommendations. Expect a classroom environment, therefore, that calls for your size-up of the situation, your analysis, what actions you would take, and why you would take them. Do not be upset if, as the class discussion unfolds, some insightful things are said by your fellow classmates that you did not think of. It is normal for views and analyses to differ and for the comments of others in the class to expand your own thinking about the case. It is to be expected that the class as a whole will do a more penetrating and searching job of case analysis than will any one person working alone. This is the power of team effort, and its virtues are that it will help you see more analytical applications, let you test your analyses and judgments against those of your peers, and force you to wrestle with differences of opinion and approaches.

To orient you to the classroom environment on the days a case discussion is scheduled, we compiled the following list of things to expect:

1. Expect the instructor to assume the role of extensive questioner and listener.

2. Expect students to do most of the talking. The case method enlists a maximum of individual participation in class discussion. It is not enough to be present as a silent observer; if every student took this approach, there would be no discussion.

3. Be prepared for the instructor to explore reasons and supporting analysis.

4. Expect and tolerate challenges to the views expressed. All students have to be willing to submit their conclusions for scrutiny and rebuttal. Each student needs to learn to state his or her views without fear of disapproval and to overcome the hesitation of speaking out. Learning respect for the views and approaches of others is an integral part of case analysis exercises. But there are times when it is OK to swim against the tide of majority opinion. In the practice of management, there is always room for originality and unorthodox approaches. Therefore, while discussion of a case is a group process, there is no compulsion for you or anyone else to cave in and conform to group opinions and group consensus.

5. Don't be surprised if you change your mind about some things as the discussion

unfolds. Be alert to how these changes affect your analysis and recommendations.

6. Expect to learn a lot in class as the discussion of a case progresses; furthermore, you will find that the cases build on one another — what you learn in one case helps prepare you for the next case discussion.

There are several things you can do on your own to be good and look good as a participant in class discussions:

1. Don't hesitate before (and after) class to discuss the case with other students though you should do your own independent work and independent thinking. In real life, managers often discuss the company's problems and situation with other people to refine their own thinking.

2. In participating in the discussion, make a conscious effort to contribute, rather than just talk. There is a big difference between saying something that builds the discussion and offering a long-winded, off-the-cuff remark that leaves the class wondering what the point was.

3. Always give supporting reasons and evidence for your views, then your instructor won't have to ask you "Why?" every time you make a comment.

4. In making your points, assume that everyone has read the case and knows what it says, avoid reciting and rehashing information in the case — instead, use the data and information to explain your assessment of the situation and to support your position.

5. Bring the printouts of the notes you have prepared to class and rely on them extensively when you express your idea. There's no way you can remember everything off the top of your head. When you have prepared thoughtful answers to the study questions and use them as the basis for your comments, everybody in the room will know you are well prepared, and your contribution to the case discussion will stand out.

References

[1] BALTZAN P. Business-driven information systems [M]. 5th ed. New York: McGraw-Hill Education, 2016: 335-336.

[2] BOORSTEIN J. Fashion victim [N]. Fortune, 2006-04-13.

[3] BOWERSOX D J., CLOSS D J., COOPER M B. Supply chain logistics management [M]. Boston: McGraw Hill International, 2002.

[4] LONG D. International logistics [M]. Boston: McGraw-Hill, 2003.

[5] ECHIKSON W. The mark of Zara [N]. Business Week, 2000-05-29.

[6] MICHEL B. Lean logistics [M]. New York: Productivity Press, 2004.

[7] PEREZ S. Inidtex profit jumps 30%, but sales concerns hit shares [N]. The Wall Street Journal, 2007-12-13.

[8] CHASE R B., AQUILANO N J., JACOBS F. R. Operations management for competitive advantage [M]. 9th ed. New York: McGraw-Hill company, 2001.

[9] BALLOU R H. Business logistics: supply chain management [M]. 15th ed. Upper Saddle River, N.J.: Pearson Prentice Hall, 2004.

[10] WRIGHT R. UPS and FedEx turn focus to consumer behavior [N]. Financial Times, 2014-08-12.

[11] CHOPRA S, MEINDL P. Supply chain management--strategy, planning and operation [M]. 4th ed. 北京：清华大学出版社，2012.

[12] MURPHY P R, Jr, KNEMEYER A. M. Contemporary logistics [M]. 11th ed. 北京：中国人民大学出版社，2017.

[13] JOHNSON P F, FLYNN A E. Purchasing and supply management [M]. 15th ed. 北京：清华大学出版社，2016.

[14] 曹洪军，阚功俭. 物流学 [M]. 北京：经济科学出版社，2009.

[15] 杨性如，万笑影. 物流英语 [M]. 上海：上海科学技术文献出版社，2003.

[16] 阚功俭，物流英语 [M]. 北京：北京大学出版社，2010.

[17] 彭岩，物流企业管理 [M]. 北京：清华大学出版社，2009.